UNIMAGINABLE WEALTH

$

The Creative Services of Hugo de Verteuil and Ian Rothwell is/are a project based arts production and consultation unit. We seek to provide prompt and practical solutions to any received or perceived problems within the cross-dynamic flows of the creative and culture industries. We will serve any public or private body and guarantee a personable and flexible specialist service. We are committed to the positive expressive potential of a speedy aesthetic founded upon a 'minimum effort = maximum effect' (MEME) work-style philosophy - but this is not to say that we are not committed to a truly socially beneficial, complex and dynamic culture. ;-)

www.cshdvir.com

http://alossofattention.tumblr.com/

www.hugodeverteuil.com

www.verywelcomemusic.com

THE CREATIVE SERVICES OF HUGO dE VERTEUIL

$

IAN ROTHWELL

$$$$$$$$$$$$$$$$$$

$$$$$$$$$$$$$$$$$$

$$$$$$$$$$$$$$$$$$

$$$$$$$$$$$$$$$$$$

$$$$$$$$$$$$$$$$$$

$$$$$$$$$$$$$$$$$$

$$$$$$$$$$$$$$$$$$

$$$$$$$$$$$$$$$$$$

$$$$$$$$$$$

This sum of US$20,200,000.00 is still sitting in my Bank and the interest is being rolled over with the principal sum at the end of each year. No one will ever come forward to claim it.

Joseph Otumba

UNIM AGINA BLE $$$$ WEAL

TH ☺

@

@

@

@

@

@

@@@   @@@

@@   @@

@@   @@

@@ @@

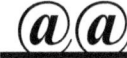

The Creative Services of Hugo de Vert i & Ian Rothwell

Unimaginabl e Wealth

$$

Felicity Nahbasa's throat burned and she had a mett allic taste in her mouth. The morphine distorted her consciousness every night. Recurring nightmares about forest fires in Australia had become normal for Felicity, but tonight she could feel the flames lick the backs of her eyelids and the smoke envelop the inside of her brain. The destructive heat seemed at one with her cancer and her chest felt like it would soon be ash.

The smell of smoke drifted into seaweed. She blinked at the sanitised hospital ward, and her consciousness shifted to the rigid bed and the sparsely decorated white room within which she had spent the last few months. Turning to her bedside table she looked at her few belongings: An elegant watch and a Louis Vee tonn handbag containing in it a slimline Apple Mak book Pro. Taking the Mak book she clicked her way into her gmail account and started to compose an email:

Dear Friend.

As you read this, please don't feel sorry for me, because, I believe everyone will die someday.

My name is Felicity Nahbasa I was recently diagnosed with Oesophagal Cancer. My illness was discovered very late, I have never been very responsible when it comes to matters regarding my health. My cancer has defied all treatment so far, and right now I have been given only a few months to live.

I fear that I have not lived a good life. I was married for forty years. I only realised how hollow our life together was after my husband died. We never really cared for anyone but ourselves and our business pursuits. Though very rich, we were never generous. Always suspicious, I have been hostile to the affection and care of friends and family. I think if I have ever cared for anything it has been my business: Myself. Lying here in this rigid hospital bed, all the luxury I have known has vanished into the ether. I am naked in the hands of fate and my wealth cannot help me. I regret my life. How stupid have I been, only now realising in my final hours that there is more to life than just wanting to have or make all the money in the world. If only I could be grant ed a second chance, I know I would live differently.

Although this is no recompense for my actions, I have willed and given most of my properties and assets to my immediate and extended family members, as well as a few close friends. I want God to be merciful. I wish to cleanse my soul somehow and meet him free of sin. I have decided to give away what remains of my unimaginable wealth to charity organizations in order to give succour and comfort to the less privil idged. I want to do at least one good deed before I leave this earth.

It is my last wish to see this money distributed to the victims of the fire outbreak in Australia and other cha...

As this last sentence began to take shape beneath her fingertips the facts of a narrative that had led to her conclusion began to form into a horrific solid shape in her mind.

$$

Dan Patrick walked through the heavily manicured gardens of the government headquarters of the Democratic Republic of Congo. As he strode past the lush vegetation the sun beat down heavy through the prehistoric trees dappling the grass beneath his feet. He stubbed his cigarette out on some gravel and entered the building. He could hear the familiar click of his secretary's heels on the polished marble – slightly faster than usual – she had clearly been waiting for him. Before he could remove his sunglasses his secretary feverishly handed him a sealed manilla envelope and ushered him in to the President's office. President Laurent Nabilla sat at his desk and seeing Patrick's arrival turned the television set on to mute. Such impromptu meetings had become a regular occurrence over the past few months. The President silently gestured towards an empty chair. As Patrick sat down, the President nodded towards the envelope.

'Have you seen it?'
'No Sir, Karen passed it to me on my way in, is it fresh?' Dan removed his sunglasses.

'Yes, new information.' Nabilla slid his antique ivory envelope knife across the desk.
'We just received it an hour ago from intelligence. It's bad Dan.'

Dan calmly sliced through the glue seal and slipped out the black and white reconnaissance photographs. It showed the area of the Congolese jungle occupied by the President's son, Joseph. He had seen this camp documented before, but in this image the rebels had clearly invested in some major arms; comprehending the heavily pixelated image Dan could clearly discern a number of RPG's and heavily armoured vehicles. It looked like the situation was about to get very very serious.

'That's some mighty firepower chief, your son has clearly invested much more in this rebellion than we thought.'
'This is no time for humour. Our forces are still heavily engaged in the south, they need all our support, but with only our current defences, I fear we will not be able to push Joseph back if he mounts an assault on the city. A

Togolese mercenary army is already on its way to swell my son's forces. We just don't have the arms Dan. I need you to arrange a swift and discreet deal with our Nigerian contact as soon as possible. It's urgent'

'I understand.'
The President opened a draw to his left and removed a second envelope. Nervously pulling on his ear he stood up and walked towards the door of his office. Dan dusted the creases from his stone-grey suit as he stood to leave. Handing Dan the envelope the President grasped his shoulder.

'Discretion Dan, please. If Joseph hears of this account . . .'
'I understand.'

He knew where to find him. Colonel Rasheidi Karesava was probably the most loyal trustworthy man he knew. Dan entered the office holding the envelope out in front of him.

'What the fuck Rasheedi, you heard about this!?' Dan says, trying to keep his anxious voice hushed.
'Of course, I heard about it earlier.'
'You know it may be too fucking late right?'
'Yes but we must place our trust in Mr Charles and Mr Creek.' Rasheedi tried to stay calm in the face of Dan's outburst.
'I'll broker the deal but I do not trust the Americans. There's no chance they can get this done in time. There's enough weaponry detailed here to wipe out half the continent. Is that his aim?!'
'Stay calm, I have the account details. The money will be transferred to one of my security firms, so if something goes really wrong it will be safe.'
'Ok, well... I'm really hungry, do you want to go get a sandwich from the canteen.'
'No thanks Dan, my wife makes my lunch.' Rasheidi holds up a plastic bag weighted down with something.

$$$

A cool Lagos breeze rippled through the open windows and for a moment the white linen curtains seemed to dance in the air. An open bottle of champagne rested in a silver container on a room-service trolley. Two glasses stood by it; one half full with a lipstick smeared rim and the other empty. The silver surface of the cooler had started to perspire a pulp-like condensation. Michael Creek ran his finger along the hard surface, catching beads of chilled water on his rough skin. Returning to the naked woman laying atop of the white linen bedsheets, he stroked his finger; clavicle to belly button. The chilly contact on her warm flesh caught her offguard, and she giggled.

'Oh Michael, can we stay here forever?'
'That's not long enough for me.'
'We rarely get to do this anymore, I still want you so bad.'
'Everything is so complicated, I don't know...' She caressed his hair and his trail of thought meandered into a cosy web of tender feeling, lost in her gentle touch he entered her.

Michael stepped out of the shower and brushesd his teeth, conscious of his meeting with Mr Charles he made sure to remove all scent of Mrs Charles' sweet perfume, spraying on his own cologne liberally. He dressed hurriedly. Kissing his sleeping lover on the cheek he carefully left the hotel room, closing the door quietly behind him. The white linen curtains continued their dancing.

$$

It was not long before he was driving down the Ibadan express road in his silver BMW. He turned off onto the Ikorodu road. Driving past the new developments he imagined the city in 2050, suspended highways weaving in and out of the skyscrapers. He took a sharp left way down into the depths of an underground car park. The lift smelled damp and he suddenly realised how sad the gifts he had brought for his daughter now seemed. He pushed the button for the 12th floor.

Jani Adams was 16 years old, she was just finishing a bowl of cheerios when the doorbell rang.

'I'll get it Mom!' She said through a mouthful of cereal and opened the door to her families tiny flat, undoing several of the many locking devices before she realised that she had forgotten to check who was calling through the peep-hole. Standing on tiptoes she glimpsed some familiar, neatly parted black hair; it was Mr Creek, a family friend who didn't visit all that often. She squeaked with excitement.
'Hey Mike, it's so nice to see you!!' She hurriedly finished removing all the locks and opened the door. 'Where have you been?'

Mr Creek accepted Jani's sudden embrace and patting her on the head replied, 'Business Jani, its always business that keeps me away from my friends. It's great to see you too, you change so much every time. But your smile stays the same.' He said as he held her by the shoulders and looked into her eyes, so similar to those he had lost himself in less than an hour ago. He blushed, and handed Jani the flowers and a wrapped gift. 'These are for you, I'm sorry I can't stay, please apologise to your parents, tell them that I will be in touch very soon.'
'But Michael . . . I thought.'
'I know I'm sorry it must be confusing but I'm afraid that I really can't stay this morning, I've just been informed that they need me urgently down-town. Look, don't worry, I'll be back in the week, we'll go out for ice cream.'
'Ah, OK. See you then.' She said, staring at her feet, struggling to return Mr Creeks affectionate glance. Mr Creek watched Jani disappear as the door closed again, and as he walked away he could hear the clunk of locks sliding back into place.

$$

The lat pull down resistance machine was in use. Mr Creek did not want to interfere with its current user to see how much longer he would be. This individual – presumably an employee of the Chevron Oil Exploration corporation - face red with concentration and teeth gritted with determination wore apple-white buds shutting him off from the outside world. It would be a very awkward interaction with someone he barely knew. Instead Mr Creek found himself gazing at the free-weights and then at his own reflection in the floor to ceiling mirror of the corporation's excellent gymnasium facility. He hadn't pumped any iron yet but he had already started to break sweat. His trainer was always on his back about his posture and how he needed to train himself to be more aware of it. Thinking about what his body looked like before moving to Lagos, he tried to look at his situation objectively. How his arms fell slightly forward and his shoulders seemed to draw in to his chest. Turning around he saw a definite curvature in his spine

'You look bad Mike.' He thought to himself.

Before he could resolve a personal pact to get fit, his mind – as it always seemed to in moments of private reflection – drifted back to the woman. Feeling a warm breeze even though he was inside a fully air conditioned gym, he could almost smell Mr Charles's wife's hair and skin as they brushed their teeth together in the hotel room bathroom, staring at each other in the mirror, considering how different they looked to themselves when they were together. Looking into this mirror now though, Michael was alone, self contained, disaffected. He meant so little to anybody in the room, he didn't even work here, he didn't recognise anybody in the gym. He had to be discreet, for the sake of the business.

He was always discreet, always careful. The phone in his gym shorts vibrated. Feeling a tremble as he unlocked the screen, he imagined her mind sharing the same intimate reminiscence he had. A text of confirmation and affirmation of their love perhaps? No. Instead of her name he saw a small C G I alarm clock dancing: He had a meeting to attend with Mr Charles.

$$$

Mr Charles' secretary smiled and lowerred her emery board as Creek approached the office. She knew him well and it was barely necessary, but nevertheless she waved her approval and sang 'Mr Creek Sir' into the intercom. Mr Charles did not respond, Creek was already opening the door to his office. Mr Charles was on the phone by the large window, one leg raised and bent to rest on the ledge. Mr Creek sat on the comfortable leather couch and waited, listening to the conversation and trying to figure out who it could be.

Mr Charles held his hand over the phone. 'The Congolese.' he said. Michael nodded.

'Could I stop you there, a close business associate of mine has just arrived. Mr Creek, you remember? Do you mind if I put you on speaker?'

Mr Creek could just about make out a muffled 'not at all' from his position on the couch and Mr Charles consequently pushed a button on the phone and returned the handset.

'Hello Mr Creek.' The phone said.
'Hello Dan.' Michael recognised the voice; it was Dan Patrick, a close personal aide to the President of the democratic republic of Congo. Creek knew what this was all about, he had seen the headlines this morning - Congolese rebels strengthen their hold in the south.

'I understand you are having a little trouble with some small time bandits, I'm sure we can assist.'
'No, Creek you don't understand. We are quite capable of dealing with the issues in the southern jungles. We urgently require assistance with an uprising in the north. This must be kept discreet. We have a large order that we need to be processed and delivered as soon as possible. We are willing to pay above and beyond the usual costs for this service. I must insist that you take the utmost care to keep this deal as secretive as possible. As always we will contact you with a number and our requirements through Agent Issssee Aywoo.'

'Does Aywoo have the information yet?'
'We passed on our requirements about an hour ago, yes. He should be on his way to you now.'
'Excellent.'
'As I have said, speed and discretion are of the utmost importance and you will be rewarded handsomely for your efforts.'
'Don't worry Mr Patrick, everything will be fine, we are well fixed to accommodate an order of this nature at the present time. We will confirm the details with you through the agent as soon as a plan has been finalised, before the end of the day. Goodbye Mr Patrick.'

Mr Charles turned off the phone and sat down as Mr Creek stood up and moved towards the desk.

'This could be good for us Charles. Can we really pull it off?'
'Well unless they are looking for a nuclear submarine, I am sure we can get what they need and quick too. Our cashay is currently full of Kalashnikovs from the Egyptian deal and Korean MK-19's and RPG's from the deal with Tiveroli.'
'And the U N?'
'Still clueless, the sanctions around the Congo are as weak as water, especially with Bahbu to smooth things through the Government account, its unbelievable how much our operation has improved since he came on board with us.'

The intercom flashed and beeped. Mr Charles pushed the speaker button.

'It's Mr Aywoo to speak to you Mr Charles.'
'Very good, send him through Janice.'
'Issssee Aywoo my good man! Excellent to see you.' Charles stood up holding out both arms graciously. Mr Creek remained seated with a pensive look on his face.
'Please, don't call me that stupid Goat Head codename, it's not really necessary in here is it.' Bahbu remained at a distance from the American men. 'Dr Bahbu will do nicely Charles, and you would do well to remember that. Michael, I trust you are well?'
'Issssee Aywoo – sorry, force of habit – Dr Bahbu.'
'Please sit down doctor. You're making me as nervous as a nun in a whorehouse.'

Bahbu sat down and flashed a look of disgust in response to the elderly American's vulgarity.

Babu was a large man, proud of his appearance and proud of his stately position within the Nigerian government. A position he routinely undermined through his dealings with Mr Charles and Creek. The fragility of this respectability only served to enhance the formality of his appearance, and as he sat, it looked as if his fastidiously pressed suit were resolutely immune to crumple. Removing his sunglasses, Bahbu placed them carefully within his breast pocket all the while maintaining unnerving eye-contact with Charles.

'You must have heard from the Congolese by now. I have the dossier.'

Bahbu handed Mr Creek an envelope.

'Its pretty routine stuff, but the price is certainly right. Its unimaginable! But some things have come to light that might make it difficult to complete the transaction through the usual channels.'
'What are you talking about? Cut to the chase man, we aren't playing cricket. Dear god!'
'Do you remember the Liberian deal from a few years back?' Dr Bahbu asked, unflinching in the face of Charles verbal assault.
'Of course and as I remember it was a tremendously smooth deal, completely above board.'
'Well I know that's how it looked to us, but there's a Mr Edward Wark, Californian I think, he's over here working with the embassy. He's investigating the Liberian military accounts and the paper trail could easily lead back to us. I've met him, he's thorough, and a regular fucking George Washington. You would be wise not to rock the boat right now, there's some rot growing. You know full well that the nature of the deal could jeopardise your security, considering that Wark will, undoubtedly will, ask to inspect your accounts. Soon.'
'Dr Bahbu, my good friend, this is your responsibility. If you can't smooth this over then why the fuck are we working with you? You have profited greatly from us, and you know your part in our relationship is to deal with matters such as this. If you can't smooth it over with this Wark fuck this time, then we are going to have to find you a different role, in the interests of maintaining our delightful business relationship. Right Michael?'

Mr Creek nodded. 'Charles look at this figure.'

Creek passed over the document. Charles rationalizing the sum silently did not respond but turned back to Bahbu.

'Thanks very much Bahbu, this is great, but if you want to get paid any more than a pre-pubescent on a newspaper round, you are going to have to put in some serious work. I understand the nature of the new situation with Wark. We will complete the transaction through the Libyans. Can you leave the country for a few days?'
'Of course, if the price is right.'
25%.
'I want 30% and not a penny less!'
25% or you're out you cheeky fuck.' Charles chuckled at his crippling of Bahbu's crystalline demeanour.
'Fine, but I'm flying first class.'
'Ha, I wouldn't expect anything less. We'll contact you Bahbu. Don't switch that pager off. Keep it fucking charged. Ha. Till then.'
'Till then Charles. Creek.'

Bahbu put his sunglasses back on, stood up, nodded at his associates and left the room, curtly closing the door behind
him.

$$

Edward Wark felt the weight of historical responsibility on his gymnasium
groomed shoulders, as he sent the final account details to the printer. He
took the paper, machine warm, and paperclipped it to the other documents
in the dossier he was compiling concerning the transactions of The Top
Military Officer's armory invoices. He locked his briefcase and left the office.
As he placed his palm neatly on the hand facsimile on the handscanner – a
ritual necessary to enter and leave the UN headquarters – his secretary
chirped:

'What's up Ed.'
'Everything.'
'What do ya mean, what's wrong?'
'Everything is wrong.'

The handscanner beeped its approval and Ed, leaving the building, observed
one of his colleagues – a formidable corporate lawyer – swiping his entry
pass and pushing through the gurney. Wark waited a moment watching the
lawyer place his briefcase and shoes on the conveyor belt and pass through
the x-ray arch. The machine beeped, he had forgotten to remove his belt.
The security guard bruskly attempted to pass his wand over the lawyer. The
lawyer already aware that his belt was the cause of this hold up tried to palm
off the security guard but to no avail. The security guard insisted on passing
the wand over the lawyer's shoulders and back, stomach, legs and groin
before saying.

'It's probably just your belt, would you mind removing it for me sir and
passing through the machine again.'

Wark waved at the lawyer as he passed by the final exit security desk with
his pass held high and left the building. The Lawyer was too distracted to
respond.

Wark headed for his vehicle, still chuckling to himself.

It was hot. Too hot. Wark was aware that he was already sweating profusely.
Though California born and bred he still couldn't adjust to the intensity of
the African summer. He put the air conditioning up to eleven and drove

slowly towards the main gates, allowing for a train of decrepit, antique buses to pass through into the compound. They were the refugee transport vehicles, headed for Ghana later in the day. "Good luck to them," he thought as he began to peel away into the streets of Monrovia. He tried to find some news on the radio but to little effect. Mostly just static and pop music, he let it play. Driving along the city streets, the wreckage of a never ending war piled up around him, he found it difficult to concentrate. He heard shots in the distance, mingling with the honking of car horns, as seemingly permanent as bird song. As the crow flies it wasn't far to the Monrovia Military Residential Compound. But he could forget about the crows, Wark was in the capital of Liberia; the streets were an apocalyptic chaos of crowds.

Eventually he arrived at his destination: A chain-linked fence furnished with barb wire. More security and more guards with guns: Wark knew them to be AK-47's. The AK-47 is a selective-fire, gas-operated 7 point 62 by 39mm assault rifle. It was first developed in the Soviet Union by Mikhail Kalashnikov, indeed it is also known as a Kalashnikov. Wark's work required a detailed knowledge of such weaponry, and as he pushed the button for the automated window of his car he thought of how even after six decades this particular automated rifle had remained the most widely used and popular assault rifle in the world. Its durability, low production cost, and ease of use had secured its place on the throne. Furthermore it had been manufactured in many countries and had seen service with armed forces as well as revolutionary and terrorist organizations worldwide.

He handed the man with the iconic weapon an envelope containing fifty American dollars through the window. The man nodded approval and waved him through into the residential compound. The sky was the colour of a cigarette stained wall and driving through the gated community was like entering a mirror. He wound his way through the dusty streets, so suddenly calm. He flipped open the folder on the passenger seat to confirm that he was approaching the correct address. After pulling up to the low detached building, he left his vehicle, feeling his sweat soaked shirt peel slowly from the leather seat.

The steps of the porch sunk as he stepped up to the door. Something reminded him that what a barbed wire fence meant to the rest of the world was a meaning worth less than nothing in Monrovia. He knocked. There was no answer. He knocked again, this time introducing a touch of aggression; still nothing. He could see a shadow moving through the thin lace curtains.

He would not shout, in other parts of the city this could get a man like him killed. Speaking calmly through the letterbox he said.

'My name is Edward Wark, I'm with the United Nations, and I just want to talk.'

The door cracked open:

'My husband is not here.'
'Do you know when he will be back?'
'No.' She snapped sharply, struggling to keep eye-contact with the American.
'Do you know where he is?'
'He died.'
'Oh. Well. I am truly sorry for your loss. When did this happen?'

Ed felt a weight form in his stomach and her eyes remained fixed on the terracotta vinyl floor.

'Can we talk about it?'

Anxious over her lack of cooperation, Ed reached into his pocket.

'What are you doing? I don't want your money. Please go away.'

Ed saw the door slowly closing and quickly stopped it with his foot.

'Please, this is urgent. I have no quarrel with your husband. I just need to know a few things. Please, this could help to put away some terrible people. Please. Tell me, how did your husband die?
'He was gunned down in Jorrck penn kin Market.'
'Why did this happen? Please help me; I am hunting the real source of all this misery.'
'Sir you don't understand, there is no source here. Everything is misery. No one brought the misery here, it just. Is.'
'But, the gun runners. Do you know anything of a Mr Creek? An American like myself.'

The door opened up eventually: 'Come in', she sighed.

Ed stepped into the house, the screen door snapped satisfyingly behind him. He followed The Widow down the narrow corridor and into a small living room at the back of the house with large open windows. The Widow gestured toward a wicker chair. Ed sat down placing his folder on the nearby table. The evening blew in on a warm breeze, gathering around them and animating the edges of the paper-clipped documents; the evidence inside impatiently waiting to be revealed.

'Would you like a drink?' The Widow asked.
'My husband and I used to enjoy a Campar ree and soda at this time'
'That would be great, thank you.'

Wark watched as the Widow took a half bottle of Campar ree from a corner cupboard and placed it on the table. 'I will be back in a moment' she said. Ed looked out onto the dry lawns of the gated community and watched as some children raced their bmx's over the crest of a hill. The raspberry red liquor shon elegantly translucent; the colour popped within the shale dust room. He knew Campar ree, a Milanese aperitif, its colour like that of children's boiled candy, its taste as bitter as gall. The Widow returned with two high ball glasses filled with ice and a litre bottle of sowder water. She took the sunrise-red liquor and poured a generous portion into each glass, it wound its way through the cubes like a Chinese dragon. He let the taste linger in his mouth before swallowing; its bittersweet sensation allowing a moment of reflective reprieve.

'Thank you, this is delicious.'

He placed his glass on the table and picked up the folder. He spread out the documents on the table and pointed to a list of account transactions and invoices.

'Your husband was in charge of buying weaponry for his garrison, were you aware of his responsibility in this area?' Wark asked.
'Of course', she responded before drinking deeply from her glass, the ice cubes clinking as she placed it back down on to the hard surface of the table. There was no coaster.

'As you know, In Liberia, the armourer is a gatekeeper. The warden of a kind of Pandora's box. It is his responsibility to make sure that his transactions are legal. Your husband never set a foot wrong in this regard I can assure you. We have investigated his government account fully and there are no discrepancies there. Your husband protected the honour of his government. But he dealt with less honourable dealers.' Wark paused a moment to take a sip of his beverage.

'We are trying to contact a Mr Michael Creek. Our investigations have led us to conclude that he sold to your husband during the civil war. Do you remember anybody with this name who was in Liberia at the time?'

The widow replenished her now empty glass.

'Yes, very much. I know Mr Creek well. He stayed here on several occasions and my husband used this building as a safe place to meet. We were protected from the rebels here at that time. We used to be safe from the rebels here.

'Do you know a Mr Charles?'

'No, but I have heard his name. I am sure that Michael Creek was working for a Nigerian mining corporation. Yes, definitely. Wait.' The widow stood up and went to a teak desk by the window. She pushed the chair aside with her hip and opened a drawer. She returned to the table and placed a pen on top of Ed's papers.

Ed Wark red aloud: 'N M C PARAH STATAL.'

'I need to confess Mr Wark. I am grateful for your visit, no one comes to see me. I have no family. They were wiped out during the civil war. Ha, I speak of it in the past tense. My father was a general of the government army and one night a rebel faction broke into our home, raped and murdered my mother and sisters and cut my father into pieces. I was the only one who survived. I hid in the walls; I stayed there for three days after the rebels left. It was my future husband who found me and nursed me back to health. He was an orphan himself.'

'Why are you telling me this? You have done nothing wrong. Your strength is astounding.'

'Don't flatter that which I resent. I am filled with rage. I want nothing more than to leave this country and its filth and suffering far far behind me. My husband was a rich man. You say he kept his business clean, but war corrupts everything it touches and he must have found some way in which to profit. Probably selling his arms on to the rebel factions after his political convictions had been corroded by the government's lies. Mr Wark, I have in herited an unimaginable wealth. I have his will, which details an unimaginable wealth, kept safe for me in a metallic box at a government storage container. I have helped you Mr Wark, you can take this evidence I have connecting Creek to my husband but. I ask you return the favour, by helping me secure my inheritance in your country. I am leaving as soon as I can. I am in extreme danger now, especially without my husband.'

The widows eyes remained fixed on the floor; the emotion disguised by her glacial expression was palpable.

Ed Wark finished his drink and considered what the widow was asking of him. 'I will help you. I agree that you have to leave, come with me tonight, I can get you to a safe camp in Ghana, we can arrange for your passage out of the country from there.'

$$

The Ron Day Voo bar at the Eko hotel; Mr Charles' choice bar to relax and unwind: Elegant but comfortable. Charles' manners were brash and loud, but here he felt anonymous, the only place in Lagos were he could be confidently American. He knew the bartenders and he knew he would get what he wanted. Creek and Charles were shown to a table in the corner of the room, they sat down on the spacious sofa style seating and Mr Creek picked up the menu. He wasn't interested in what he would have to drink, he already knew what he wanted. Distracting himself with the menu and choice of beverage would, he figured, delay the painful conversation he could feel bubbling, lava-like, beneath the crust of the cordial environment within which he and his associate currently resided. The menu was laminated ox-blood red to pastel-yellow sunrise fade and Mr Charles face was sunburnt arrogance.

'What's your poison Mike?', Charles asked patronisingly.
'Not sure. Gimme a second won't you?'
'Ha. I see you as a Pina Colada guy.' Charles guffawed. 'Anyway gimme that menu.' Charles snatched the menu and slapped it down on the glass table-top through which Creeks nervous brogues were visible.
'Bourbon son? I'll order us two large ones, two rocks, nice.'
'Nah, I'm gonna go for a Negroni.'
'Ha you call yourself an American Mike?' Charles scoffed, loosening his tie and rolling his sleeves up, after carefully removing his sliver golf-ball design cufflinks – placing them neatly in his wallet.
'Coincidentally, Charles, the Negroni is a derivation of the Americano cocktail...'
'Hey Mike, I did not ask for a lecture ok, I'm not here to listen to Michael fucking Creek's history of the world!' Charles interrupted with a snort of laughter. Creek ignored this, allowing himself to indulge for a moment in his superiority, his impeccable knowledge of a subject in which the self-styled omnipotent Mr Charles was wholly ignorant.
'Regardless Charles, the Americano was – and still is for that matter – a delicious and refreshing drink, made popular by American libertarians who flocked to Europe during prohibition. It was invented by Gasspar Campar ree, the inventor of the Campar ree aperitif which is the main ingredient of the Americano. Ironically Campar ree was legal in America during prohibition as it was classed as a medicinal product, not an alcoholic beverage. It is a little on the light side however, and definitely too light for

this time of the evening, but that's why we have the Negroni, which was created in the bar of the Hotel Bagglioni on the Arno river in Florence Italy in 1925 when Count Camillo Negroni decided that the Americano was too tame a drink for his tastes and asked the barman to spike his Americano with a splash of Gin.'

'FUCK THAT MIKE. I did not ask for your shit history. That means nothing to me. I don't care, let me have bourbon, two rocks. DONE.' Charles snapped his fingers crudely in the direction of a waiter floating at the perimeter of their table.

'Waitress, we'll have one bourbon, two rocks – nice – and whatever this guy wants.'

'A Negroni for me sir, on rocks, the largest ice-cubes you got.' Creek asked, self-satisfyingly sitting back in the chair.

'You still getting time to play any golf Charles?'

'Yes Mike, not enough though, although Bahbu and I played a few holes last week. You know he has a scratch handicap! Ha, I had no idea until he struck that first ball. Straight as an arrow down the fairway!'

'Unbelievable, Bahbu it seems is a man of many talents.'

'Yes he is Mike, yes he is. We were harsh on him earlier, he is a man of repute, but when he works with us he has a role and he needs to know it. Our business relationship, by its very nature, is tense, and rests on trust. We need to feel secure that he is taking care of things at his end in the Government office. When he said that bull kkrap about this Wark guy I nearly lost my shit. Trying to scare us or something. I thought he knew what he was doing, but it seems something is slipping. In many ways our little enterprise rests on his shoulders, he can't know that, obviously, but this Wark character though. It makes me think, not everything has been as neatly concealed as we might have liked to think.'

'Its been sitting on me too Charlie, I have some serious concerns. Can we talk?' A black cocktail napkin fluttered onto the table, 'Your Negroni sir,' 'Thank you.'

'Cheers Mike.' Charles raised his glass and caramel brown met raspberry red with a clink.

Charles threw his head back and poured the whole glass of bourbon into his mouth, clicking at the waitress mercilessly as he did so. He spun his fingers round in a circle, the director wanted to play the scene out again. Michael sipped; an initial spike of gin and campar ree mellowed, he tried to concentrate on the sensation, willing it to linger on his tongue as he watched the waitress walk away.

'Plainly, can we talk plainly?'

'What do you have to say to me Mike?'

'If this Wark guy is really looking into Liberia it won't be long until he finds exactly what he needs to send me down. You know as well as I do that that deal wasn't really tight.'

'What are you saying, you think we're cooked?'

'Not yet, but it's a close run thing. Look, I know for a fact that The Top Military Officer we sold to was assassinated last week in Monrovia, If Wark is looking into his special accounts now then we'll be feeling the heat from him, soon. Look, there is nothing that you can't get out of here, we both know that. I dealt with this account directly and none of it implicates you as far as Wark is concerned, but if he gets to me then we are both finished, I can't possibly hide everything from a UN investigation.'

'Think about what you are saying carefully Mike, we have other things to be concerned about. Don't you realise how big the Congolese thing is? I need you for that man, you can't do this to me. This is serious money, the Congolese are serious people to be playing with, its not just the money we have to lose, its our fucking guts! You don't know what they are capable of, we're locked in to this now.'

'I know but the longer we wait.'

'No Mike, I can not allow this to happen.' The atmosphere between them changed dramatically. Mr Charles large frame was suddenly upright at the table, his hand gripped the rocks glass tightly and his eyes, brutal and expressionless, unblinking, like a great white shark, locked on to Michael.

'You will finish this deal with me. You will benefit and I will benefit and then we can have this conversation.' Charles explained carefully, his voice like a judge. This was his law, and any deviance would not be tolerated.

'We have an accord then?'

'What can I say Charles, what must be done must be done.' Michael, took his glass, but this time he didn't sip. Mr Charles great white shark face remained unaffected.

'Charles, I'm going, I'll see you tomorrow. We'll arrange for Bahbu's transit to Liberia.' Mr Charles demeanour broke as he got up to meet Michael's hand. He genially pulled Mike into an embrace, clapping him on the back.

'Don't worry about it Mike, it's gonna be good.'

Hurriedly Mr Creek threw down 2500 naira, another 1000 for a tip, and left. Mr Charles remained. Throwing another bourbon down his throat he reached for the inside pocket of his navy blue blazer. He held his Blackberry mobile phone in the palm of his hand, and dialled a number. Straight to voicemail: 'I will need your services; you know which number to call.'

Then he hung up.

$$

In a shady clearing, King Arah wee sat on a plastic chair, his golden jewellery and crown glinting in the bowabab tree dappled sunlight. This broad-trunked tropical tree was of the silk-cotton family, native to Africa. It has an edible acidic fruit resembling a gourd and its bark was used in making paper, cloth and rope. Indeed the king's distinctive golden headdress was partly made of this bark, and surrounded by his tribe he spoke through the traditional speaker who held a staff topped with a big carved wooden figurine, his face painted with white chalk polka dots.

'We are gathered here, men, wives and children, to celebrate and protect the courage and bravery of our warriors. Tomorrow they will leave us to fight in the Democratic Republic of Congo. Their success there will bring great wealth. Unimaginable wealth to this tribe and we shall all prosper for generations to come.'

$$

Emmanuel Attipoe scratched his chest, the long bullet belts lay heavy on his shoulders and dug in to his skin. He remembered the screening of Rambo first Blood that he had watched with friends in Lome last year and smiled to himself, 'I'll give you a war you won't believe,' he chuckled. A friend slapped him on the arm and pointed to the corner that the jeep was approaching. It looked to Emmanuel like an overgrown Termites nest but as the jeep turned he could see clearly a mound of naked bodies. The jeep slowed down as they approached the stad de martre, the ron day voo for his company with the forces of the rebel leader and son of the current president, Joseph Nabilla. Men wearing fatigues, red armbands and berets shouted and waved as they approached. The driver stopped the engine and Emmanuel jumped over the side of the vehicle with the rest of his unit. Other jeeps and armoured trucks were pulling into the stadium car-park now, and the familiar faces of his tribesmen began piling out of them. The waving and shouting had not stopped, the French language of the Congolese sounded like obscure noise to Emmanuel at first, but soon it became clear that an urgent communication was at hand. 'Its happening now.' He understood, 'Weapons over here!' His commander called to the unit to gather around the munitions vehicle and the crowd of men followed loyally. A Congolese soldier began furiously throwing A K 47's from the back of the vehicle into the crowd and another dumped boxes of bullets at the Togolese mercenaries feet, another distributed Rocket Propelled Grenade Launchers, flash grenades and other explosive ordnance. After taking as many grenades as he could fit in his pockets, Emmanuel followed the rest of his unit back to the jeep, now he really felt like Rambo.

The convoy split; the jeep pulled away down a residential street, the buildings decorated with bullet holes. Emmanuel began to discern the particular rattle of automated gunfire, breaking the uncanny silence of the city. The jeep slowed to a halt as they approached a corner gas station, deserted. A shout ordered him back over the side of the vehicle and he moved as one with his unit onto the opposite side of the road. The presidential mansion was half a mile away but the sound of the gunfire felt strangely close. Following their commander, the unit ran, hunched and scattered, through a labyrinth of dusty alleyways.

When they arrived at the thick stone walls surrounding the presidential mansion the commander ordered the men behind him to fire 3 rockets into the masonry, blasting vast chunks of matter metres into the air and creating a gaping entrance into the once heavily manicured gardens. Sirens screamed and the president's defense machine gun outposts jerked into life, directing their fire at the hole, desperately seeking targets. The commander barked an order into the crowd of warriors behind him and Emmanuel was passed an RPG launcher by a soldier in front of him. He was boosted onto the low balcony of a nearby home and swiftly climbed up onto the roof, swivelling into position. He took aim and swiftly dispatched a rocket; it roared upwards on a pillar of fiery smoke, stabbing through the cloudless sky before falling directly into the machine gun outpost, annihilating it with unerring accuracy. 'I'll give you a war you won't believe.' Emmanuel muttered as his friends cheered and shouted.

Emmanuel jumped down and ran forward through the hole in the wall with the other men, all shouting and firing scattered shots in the direction of the mansion. They could hear a cacophony of gun rattle coming from the other side of the building, the tactical split had paid off; their route through to the building was barely guarded at all as Emmanuel's shot had taken out the only thing that prevented their access. Emmanuel raised his AK47 and set off at a sprint towards the mansion, knowing his comrades would be close behind and that the capture of the building would earn them great reward. He wove a zig zag course towards the entrance, pools of burning fuel and wrecked machinery forcing him into frustrating detours. After years of creeping through the Togolese forests it was a cathartic release of his fury to be amidst such brutality. The air was thick with death. Bullets whipped the ground around Emmanuel's feet. The defence from the front had obviously split. 'The roof!' he heard someone shout, seeing Government soldiers firing at him furiously from the windows and corners of the building. He could not slow down, his feet carried him all the way as if guided by fate. He stormed up the steps leading to the back entrance shooting three guards in one swathe of hot led.

He knelt down below a window ledge and pulled off one of the bullet belts that hung across his shoulders, noticing the many deep red pock marks that flecked his naked chest. As Emmanuel pushed the now fully loaded clip back into position he heard a voice from inside the building shout, 'RPG!' this time there was no language barrier. He shouted at the men running up the stairs to fall back and take cover. As soon as the message was understood the rocket exploded gouging out a great tayre in the back wall, just metres from Emmanuel's position. The noise was deafening, Emmanuel could see tiny shards of glass flying through the air around him, he could feel them cutting into his skin, but eerily could not hear their twinkling return to ground. 'Move in!!' Emmanuel silently screamed, jumping into the window and firing viciously on the group of startled soldiers before him.

As Emmanuel stared into a lifeless room, bodies limp on the rubble floor, he stopped, apprehended by its peculiar calm and revelled in his superiority. Adrenaline locked in soon enough and he climbed through the window, breaching the mansion. His comrades rushed in through the settling smoke of umber ash but were confronted by their next obstacle; a large iron door, like something you would see protecting a safe in a bank. Calling the men to stand back he carefully rolled a grenade at its hinge. 5, 4, 3, 2, 1: The blast hit his ears like a freight train and the door disappeared into heavy smog. Lethal shrapnel scythed the air. Emmanuel felt a dagger slice through his hip. He expected pain but instead felt a total loss of sensation, which seemed to him doubly terminal. Falling to his feet he breathed heavily, gulping in the air like it was water. Others fell, some did not and entered the doorway. He watched as their groaning bodies faded into smoke.

$$

From the window of the Presidents bedroom Dan Patrick fired seven deafening shots from his desert eagle into the throng of rebels mounting the front steps of the presidential mansion below. He looked out across the city and in that moment he knew that everything his government had worked for was lost. He crouched below the ledge and said loudly; 'Nabilla, all is lost, the rebels are through, they are on the steps, we have to leave for the helicopter, NOW!'
'No Dan, the hell I'm leaving, I will not surrender to my own son, one of us must die today.'

Nabilla stood up from his desk and opened the mahogany cabinet behind him. He removed his custom gold plated AK47. The sun glinted on its surface and lit his face with a golden flare revealing a steely expression. He loaded his weapon. 'Rasheidi, what do you say? Are you with me?' The president shouted. Rasheidi fired a salvo through the window. 'I am loyal to the end sir, but we are all doomed if we stay. I say we fall back.' Dan Patrick looked towards his friend. Rasheidi, crouching now, nodded back. Patrick whirled on his heels and pointed his gun at the presidents forehead.

'We are leaving sir, you can stay if you must but the helicopter is coming with me.'
'Traitor.' Nabilla seethed through clenched teeth, his steely expression melting into something irrational, crazed even. The president raised the AK47 slowly to his shoulder. Rasheidi moved from the window and pointed his gun at the President. 'Don't do it Nabilla, at least one of us is leaving you here.'
Saying nothing the president walked calmly towards the window, followed by Patrick and Rasheidi's muzzles. 'Goodbye. Its been a pleasure,' The President uttered. Patrick low erred his weapon and waved to Rasheidi, running towards an open door at the back of the room and up a set of metal stairs.

The door to the president's bedroom fell flat. As the the blistering light of the flash grenade saturated his senses, Nabilla swivelled and fired his weapon in vain at the group of soldiers rushing in to his bedroom. It was too late, he felt bullets rip like fire through his torso and falling back against the window he felt life leaving him. His head knocked coldly on the parquet floor. Blood flowed out of his temple and his heart stopped. The Togolese warriors cheered. They had neutralised their target and they were now heroes. However their cheers were soon deafened by a thick scream that pierced the air, a rocket smashed through the window, incinerating the room and everything in it.

Patrick burst through the door at the top of the flight and ran hunched over towards the helicopter, the blades spinning above his head. He climbed into the open side of the vehicle, followed by Rasheidi. 'We are leaving, NOW!' He shouted at the driver. 'But sir. I have orders from the President. ' Patrick raised his gun over the drivers seat, 'Now.' He said, firmly.

As the helicopter left the ground Patrick turned his head back into the cargo area. Rasheidi sat weeping against a box of ammunition, his head in his hands. Patrick pulled out the mobile phone from his inside jacket pocket and dialled a number. An American voice greeted him cheerfully. He shouted over the noise of gunfire and whirring, 'The deal is off Charles, it's over.'

As he hung up, snapping the phone back into place, he realised his mistake. "Rashedi, the money! Where is it?"
"Its lost Dan," he sobbed. "I had it transferred into a safety deposit box at my security firm headquarters. The president's son will be seizing all our properties. There is no hope."
"How long do we have before he finds it?"
"2 days at the most, its not worth it."
"Not if I can help it." Dan whipped his laptop computer from his shoulder bag, opened it hurriedly and began to compose an email:

Dear Sir,

SEEKING YOUR IMMEDIATE ASSISTANCE. Please permit me to make your acquaintance in such an informal manner. This is necessitated by my urgent need to reach a dependable and trust worthy foreign partner. This request may seem strange and unsolicited but I crave your attention and pray that you view my request seriously. My name is Dan Patrick and I am from the Democratic Republic of Congo. I am one of the closest aides to the former President of the Democratic Republic of Congo, Laurent Nabilla: In blessed memory may his soul rest in peace. Due to Nabilla's military campaign to force out the rebels in my country, I and some of my colleagues were instructed to go abroad to purchase arms and ammunition worth an unimaginable sum. President Nabilla was today killed in a bloody shoot-out, the day before we were scheduled to travel out of Congo. The funds – for the time being – have been secured in a private security company owned by another former aide to the president, Colonel Rasheidi Ka resava. The security of the said amount is presently being threatened as we anticipate the arrest and seizure of all properties owned by former government employees. In view of this we need a reliable and trustworthy foreign partner who can assist us in moving this money out of our country. We have sufficient contacts to move the fund under Diplomatic Cover to a security company in Europe in your name. The Diplomatic Baggage will be marked and will not pass through normal customs or airport screening and clearance. Our inability to move this money out of Congo through more official channels is the result of our lack of trust in western governments whom we assume to relinquish all ties with the late President and our government. Though we have neither seen nor met each other, the information we gathered from an associate who has worked in your country has encouraged and convinced us that with your sincere assistance, this transaction will be properly handled with honesty and success. The said money is a state fund and therefore requires total confidentiality. Thus, if you are willing to assist us in moving this fund out of Congo, you can contact me through my email address. Please provide me with your telephone number, fax number and personal information. This will enable us to discuss the modalities and what will be your share (percentage) in assisting us. I must use this opportunity and medium to implore you to exercise the utmost discretion in keeping this matter extraordinarily confidential. Whatever your decision I will await your prompt response.

Thank you and God Bless.

Best Regards,

Mr Dan Patrick

$$$

Emmanuel awoke. The last thing he remembered was the chilly sensation of removing the spoon from his grenade. What followed he did not know. He felt the familiar touch of grass on his skin, looking around he soon realised he was back at the Stadium, the air thick with conversation and pain. He turned his head, and through itching eyes he could see the twisted, bloody face of one of his brothers in arms. The pain hit Emmanuel hard and he slipped back into deathly sleep.

$$

Emmanuel awoke again. This time it was not grass he could feel in his back, but the lumps of a mattress he knew well. He stared up at the network of cracks in the ceiling, the desert landscape of his childhood day-dreams. The pain was like a venom pulsing; he couldn't move. A voice from the corner of the room.

'Emmanuel, you are awake at last!'
'Mother, is that you?'
'Of course, be calm my son, you are home now, its over'

His mother approached the bed and stood over him, placing a warm hand on his cheek.

'I am so glad to have you back, I am very lucky, barely any of the men returned.'

Emmanuel's mother turned and walked through the open door into the kitchen area. Emmanuel could hear the comforting sound of familial activity, the wooden spoon clunking on the side of the metal saucepan. She returned with a steaming bowl of maize porridge, topped with a mixture of curried okra and goat meat.
'Here son, you must eat' she said, placing the bowl on the bed side table, and helping her son up into a sitting position. She raised a spoon to his lips

'You have been unconscious for two days. The military doctors in the Congo dressed your wounds, they say you will be okay, the shrapnel was easily removed.'

His body burned.

'It hurts ma.'
'Don't worry, rest easy, we still have some morphine left.'

He swallowed a mouthfull of what he knew in his heart was a delicious meal, but he could only taste the iron that had saturated his taste receptors. He breathed heavily.

His mother took the needle and pushed it into her sons left arm and closed the gap between the plunger top and the capsule. A tear rolled down her cheek, she knew the time would come when she would have to disclose the true horror of his injury, his hip was shattered, the doctors had already removed his leg. Emmanuel quivered.

'Emmanuel!!' A faceless voice shouted from outside.
'Not now, you must rest,' Emmanuel's mother said firmly as her son reacted with a jerk, moving her hand to his chest and pushing him lightly, he submitted, morphine numb, back into the mattress.

The door thwacked against the thick wall of the room. Three men entered, Togolese warriors. Through the dull haze of the painkiller Emmanuel recognized the soldier who lay beside him at the Stadium.

'Friends,' he murmured, barely audible.

The warrior spoke - 'We must speak to Emmanuel Mrs Attipoe, alone, it is extremely urgent'
'Not now. Please, my son is very weak, he must sleep.'
'I am sorry Mrs Attipoe but you must leave now.' The warrior took Emmanuel's mother by the arm and calmly led her out of the room closing the door behind him.

'Emmanuel, we are glad to see you are awake, brother.'
'What happened to us?' Emmanuel whispered.
'After you breached the mansion we stormed the presidents office. We won Emmanuel! but at a grave cost. The front group fired a rocket into the room and our group was annihilated. I was at the back of the crowd, I lost an eye to the shrapnel.'
'How many made it back?'
'About twenty of us, brother. Most of whom will never walk again. It was a disaster.'
'Tell him about Arah wee,'
'Arawi has kept all the Congolese treasure for himself. It should be ours Emmanuel! He is corrupt, the tribe will never see a penny for our blood, while you lie here the king is furnishing himself in glory. No recompense has been offered, for my eye, for you with your leg!'

It took all Emmanuel's strength to lift his left hand from his side to where his right leg used to be. In the moment of realisation his pain was replaced by pure terror, and a flush of memory as he thought back to the moment of crazed fury that had guided him to take the mansion alone. The strong leg that had carried him then was now void space.

'We cannot let him get away with this Emmanuel, the remaining warriors are angry brother. All the survivors have agreed, we are going to poison the king tonight, him and his wretched coward son Jack Thompson. We need your approval to make it unanimous, the tribe will be ours.' The warrior lay a sympathetic hand on Emmanuel's shoulder. Emmanuel turned to look at his friend and nodded.

'Do it.'

$$

Mr Charles had learnt not to get involved in civil conflict whilst working in Africa. He knew he could not become tied to any particular leader as positions of power were never secure here. Fortunately though there was always someone else, and it was without hesitation that he arranged for communications to be made with the late President Nabilla's son Joseph, now occupying the seat of power in the Democratic Republic of Congo.

Joseph Nabilla sat in his father's office with his feet on the desk idly watching TV whilst fondling the gold-plated AK 47.

The speaker phone on the desk buzzed into static action and an American spoke; 'Is this Joseph Nabilla?'
'It is, to whom am I speaking?' Joseph asked lazily, his concentration fixed on the resplendent gold weapon.
'My name is Mr Charles, I would like to take this opportunity to congratulate you on your recent rise to power. It was a very impressive campaign and I am sure you will be a truly great leader of your country.'
'Thank you Thank you, but why would an American be calling to praise me?'
'Well, as a business associate of your late father I am very interested in the future of my involvement in the Democratic Republic of Congo, and do not wish to sever ties with your great nation. I have a business venture you might be interested in.'
'Carry on please.' Jospeh turned the TV on to mute, and lay the AK 47 down on the desk.
'We were scheduled to deliver a wealth of arms to the Kinshasa barracks to aid with your father's supression of your rebellion. This deal was obviously left unfinished, but we have already set in motion the logistics of the transaction. A sum was agreed, but we would be willing – in consideration of recent events – to offer you the whole inventory for a reasonable discount, if you agree to go ahead with the transaction as we had previously planned. We know where the money assigned by the late president was hidden, and we will – should you show us evidence of your loyalty – reveal the whereabouts of this unimaginable sum.'
'How do you expect us to show you this loyalty?'
'You will send an emissary to Libya to meet with an Agent Issy Aywoo, with the full discounted price in cash. Aywoo will swiftly arrange for the arms to be delivered and will disclose the whereabouts of the money stored in safekeeping by the former government. What d'you say Jo?'

'Why don't you just take the money for yourself?'

'Well it's a novel idea Jo, but I am a businessman, not a looter. The money is no use to me unless it can be processed correctly, for this reason we need cash or diamonds. Look if you aren't interested I am sure that the rebels in the south would be grateful for the discounted weaponry and the payoff after they loot Kinshasa's security companies, holding your head high on a stick above their heads. That is unless the cash falls back into the hands of the surviving aides loyal to your father. I wonder what they might choose to do with the money? A holiday in the Bahamas perhaps? Or maybe they will want to buy a nuclear warhead from me and blow your impudent ass away.'

'So I have no choice?'

'Welcome to politics son.' Charles chuckled. 'Our Agent will be in room 243 at the Hotel Corinthia in Tripoli at noon in two days time. There will be a two hour window for the meeting and transaction to take place, after that we will be taking our business elsewhere. Your emissary will travel alone. I trust that I don't need to inform you of the danger you will bring to yourself and your countrymen if you try anything untoward. I have friends everywhere and I hope for your sake that you are now one of them. Goodbye Jo.'

The phone clicked and emitted a hollow drone. President Joseph Nabilla sat back in the leather desk chair and laughed, spinning the seat around in circles with his feet.

$$

In an office one thousand one hundred and eight point seven four miles away:

"Babu, pack your bags and get your ass to Tripoli, the plane leaves in three hours. You'll love The Hotel Corinthia, I've read some great reviews."

$$

Jack Thompson raced his Jeep Patriot MK74 though border control at Noway, gaining entry into the Ivory Coast through Ghana. He was on the run. He had found his fathers body two nights ago: bloodshot eyes wide open as if on pause after witnessing something truly horrific, with white foam spewing from his mouth onto the pillow.

He hadn't joined the ritual victory feast that evening such was the guilt he felt. He couldn't stomach the ashen faces of his tribesman: He had not joined the soldiers on their assignment in Congo despite being the same age as most of the young warriors. When the troops returned with the news of their company's massacre his instincts told him that nothing would ever be the same again. Evidently this minor abuse of power had nearly cost him his life anyway. He had returned to his father's home late that evening after visiting the whorehouses of Lome, to witness his father and mothers undignified demise. He removed the key attached to a silver necklace around his father's neck. After using it to open the trapdoor to the household cellar, he removed the large metallic box containing the unimaginable reward his tribe had been given for their services in The Democratic Republic of Congo. He grabbed the money and ran.

Only whilst driving through the vast Palm plantations of the Ivory Coast did Jack come to realise the ramifications of his actions. The tribesmen were not going to accept his escape and theft of their only chance of a prosperous future. He would have to assume he was being followed. Taking a sharp left off the main highway the GPS machine guiding him to Abidjan snarled at him: 'You are going the wrong way'. Jack swiftly unplugged the machine, glad to be free from its crude bit-crushed computer generated voice. It would be all right, he vaguely knew the way to the capital; his father's old friend Dr Angbozan Wattre, a cocoa import export man resided there. He had made this trip many times before. But always at leisure.

He arrived at the house of Dr Wattre in the early afternoon; a strong wind was picking up and the sky was growing steadily jaundiced and cloudy, but still it was warm enough not to wear a jacket. Dr Wattre's elegant townhouse was in the wealthy district of Abidjan. He parked his car and thought about the chaos that would break the tranquillity of the area should his pursuers find him. Checking his reflection in the wing mirrors he put this out of his mind and went to ring the door bell. A moment later he heard female footsteps approach the door. It opened. A beautiful young woman, about 21 years old, opened the door holding a glass of lipstick pink rose wine. She stood there hand on cocked hip and looked at him with a peculiar expression.

'Who are you? I know you...don't I?' She exclaimed.
'Ha, don't you remember!?' Jack removed his sunglasses.
'Its me Jack... Jack Thompson?' He enquired.
'Oh my god, Jack Thompson. Its been so long.' She stared at him, willing him to respond but he did not, Sarah broke the awkward silence, turning and shouting:
'Daddy, its Jack Thomson and the Arawi's. Come down quick. And come in won't you Jack. God its hot outside, come in come in, we've got air conditioning in here!'
Jack entered the house, clutching the metallic box to his chest.
'Wait Sarah...I have come alone. I have come with some bad news. My.'
'Alone! How odd. Please sit down, god. Would you like a glass of wine?'
'I fear you are not listening to me properly, but I will take a glass.' As Sarah poured Jack a glass of wine, Dr Wattre entered the room:
'Jack, my boy, fantastic to see you! It's been forever! Why did you stop coming with your father to visit me? It's hard going for a man in a house full of women you know" he chuckled. "Come here and give me some love.' The giant elderly man held out his white be-suited arms wearing a genial expression completely at odds with Jack's inner turmoil. His long white beard brushed jacks cheek coarsely as they embraced.
'To what do we owe this unexpected pleasure? And where is your father?'
'I am afraid I am the bearer of bad news' Jack said quietly. 'Dr, my father was killed three nights ago, poisoned to death by his own tribesmen.' A silence. Sarah lowered her wine glass and placed it on the coffee table. Dr Wattre shuddered, stunned by the news and fell back into an open armchair.

'I can't believe it, he was sitting in this very room less than a month ago.' He put his head in his hands.
'The tribe were greatly angered by the events in the south. My father took a risk and paid with his life.'
'What about you? How did you escape?'
'I was not at the feast, I knew in my gut that something was wrong. I went into Lome and when I returned late that night I found his body and that of my mother. I just got in the jeep and ran.'

'But here!!?' Dr Wattre shouted, suddenly angry. "You would bring the wrath of your tribe onto my house!! How stupid can you be?"

'Please doctor, I am sorry, I didn't know what else to do, there is nowhere else for me to go, I am throwing myself at your mercy. I can assure you, I took all the necessary precautions to throw the tribe off my trail. They can't have followed me here.'

'Don't be so foolish, you know they will catch up with you eventually.'

'Please, I need your help!' Jack blurted. 'I am carrying my father's treasure. I need to hide it somewhere, I was thinking that maybe we could come to some kind of arrangement. I would be willing to invest.'

The doctor, standing now, interrupted him 'Look Jack if we are going to talk we have to go somewhere else, I can't jeopardise the safety of my daughter.'

Turning to pick up his jacket and briefcase from the breakfast counter he spoke firmly;

'Sarah, please, go to the beach house for the night.' Sarah looked at her father, complacently sipping her wine.

'NOW!' The doctor shouted, grasping her arm and pulling her out of the chair lightly.

'Okay, I'm going!' His daughter squeaked, rushing out of the room, her high heels clicking on the tiled floor.

Doctor Wattre looked at the cold metal box at Jack's feet, as if noticing it for the first time. 'Okay Jack, we will go down town, I know a café where we can discuss this properly.'

$$

Jack Thompson and Doctor Wattre travelled silently into the city. The doctor directed Jack through a network of close back-streets and out onto a busy high street.

'Here, turn into this alley, we will park the car here.'

Jack brought his vehicle to a stand-still by some large refuse containers at the back of this dark dead-end, and the odd couple made their way back out into the light of the street.

They entered the busy café unknowingly.

'I'll grab those seats,' Wattre said, pointing to a corner booth.
'Order me a black coffee won't you?'
'Of course.' Jack replied taking his place in the queue.

Minutes later he was sat down with Wattre and two black coffee's, his back facing the door. He took a sip.

'That's good coffee.'
'How much do you have Jack?' Wattre asked sternly, staring directly into the eyes of his young friend.
'Too much Dr. It's. Unimaginable.' He replied. 'I want you to put it to use within your company. In exchange you will cut me in for 80% of the profits. I will become majority shareholder, the heir to the throne that you never had. Your an old man Doctor. I assure you that this investment will make you more money than you have ever made in your life.'
'I like you Jack but do you really think I have no pride at all? 80%? With no credentials!? Your an amateur. 30% is far too low a price for my life Jack, we go 50/50 or you are on your own. I don't need a sleeping partner.'

Wattre sipped his coffee and looked up. A man wearing a white t-shirt and jeans brushed past the booth on his way out the door, take-away cup in hand. The man turned as he left to return the Dr's gaze, Wattre noticed his black eye-patch and something turned in his stomach. Dangerous thoughts filled his mind. Trying to remain calm, he looked back to Jack.

'I think we should leave soon.'
'But, we've only just got the coffee's?'

Wattre pulled his brief case up onto the table and undid the two clasps simultaneously with a satisfying 'click'. Removing a paper from one of the silk-lined inner wallets he closed the case again.

'I think we can do business Jack. Here is the address of my attorney,' he said, pointing to the letter head. 'His office is a couple of miles away. You will go there now, alone, take the jeep, but be careful.' He began writing something in elegant script at the bottom of the letter. 'I will ring my lawyer from here to inform him that you are on your way, and to draw up the necessary documents for the transferral of your funds.' He stopped writing. 'This is the telephone number and address of the beach house where Sarah will be. I want you to go to the Lawyer, finish the deal and then call me here. After it is done I never want to see you again. I will transfer you r returns to a P.O box of your designation once you are settled somewhere far away. The rest is up to you. Personally I think you should leave the continent completely. Your father has destroyed a tribe and created a desperate gang, god knows what punishments they have in store for you.' Jack looked blankly back at the Doctor. 'I understand.' Jack folded the letter, slipped it into his pocket, and stood up, taking his coffee with him. He picked up a take-away cup from the stack at the corner of the service desk and poured the still warm drink into the receptacle and left.

He turned left, scanning the streets for pursuers. Stopping at an electrical box he placed his cup on the rough pickle-green surface and removed a half bottle of highland park scotch whisky from his inside breast pocket. There was a strange moment of total silence just before it happened, a meta-second of calm to balance the chaos of the café's explosion. The whole world seemed to wretch with the noise and destruction of the bomb, and then smoke, dust, screams of pain. Jack Thompson stood, staring into the mess, his take-away coffee thrown half way across the street in fear, the bottle of whisky held tightly in his hand. He took a quick swig and ran for the car.

$$$

The queue at departures moved slowly at Murt allah Muhammed International Airport. Dr Goron yoh Bahbu impatiently shuffled as he looked at his gold wrist-watch. He stared as an overweight woman struggled to remove her shoes without sitting down. He sniggered. Eventually it was his turn to enter through the great portal into the departure lounge. He looked for his man and found him waving hurriedly. He walked towards the officer and a silent moment of recognition passed between them. Bahbu removed his shiny black leather shoes and placed them on the conveyor belt with his briefcase and belt, watching the objects pass into the machine.

He walked through the portal in silence and stood waiting for his belongings. The officer operating the x-ray machinery waved over her colleague, the man on the other side approached the screen and looked at the items of concern. He looked back to Bahbu who nodded expectantly, and briskly ordered his female colleague to pass the baggage through. Bahbu sternly collected his things. As he walked away a wide smile broke out on his face and he buttoned his jacket with his free hand.

"You are good Charles, very good indeed." He said to himself.

An hour later he was boarding the plane to Libya. He was led to his seat in first class by an attractive stewardess who took his briefcase and stowed it in the overhead bin. Babu settled comfortably into the leather couch and thought about the champagne he would receive when the plane was in the air.

"I love champagne" he thought.

He buckled his seat belt and lying back into the cushioned head rest, closed his eyes.

$$

It was 6 pm in Lagos. Michael Creek lay on his bed trying to read Flaubert's 'Madame Bowvery.' He sighed, he just couldn't do it. He couldn't read anything but the newspaper and the documents necessary for his work any more. It just didn't seem worth the time. Placing the book closed and flat by his side he brought his hands to rest behind his head and thought of Mrs Charles. She had given him the book as a gift just before their last meeting. He wondered when they would see each other again, he needed to see her, his mind was continually drifting into memories of the nights he had spent in her arms, the only time in his life that he had felt truly at peace. The bedside phone rang, abruptly disturbing his repose. He answered, it was Mr Charles, "How appropriate," He thought to himself.

'Creek, how are ya?'
'You know Charles, taking it easy, trying to keep a low profile, remember?'
'Ha, you worry too much buddy. We haven't heard anything back about that little detective yet have we? He's probably running into all the walls I have built around the borders, he can't touch us, don't worry about it. Say, you didn't hear from Bahbu yet did you?'
'He rang me from the departure lounge a few hours ago, why?'
'Oh nothing, he'll be fine, just settling into the hotel room now I should imagine. Probably spending all my money on room service, liquor and hoares the bastard. Anyway, I'm calling to confirm that you can be in the office over the next two days to handle any incoming trade. I have to take a trip to Sierra Leone with the lawyer, Agahbi, you remember? To arrange a transfer. You understand?'
'Sure Charles, I remember. I will be there. I can handle it. Keep me informed okay?'
'Yeah, well maybe I would if I thought it was worth my while.' Charles said, poisonously.
'Goodnight Mike.'

Michael hung up the phone and his attention reverted back to expedia.com, the website lighting up his computer screen. He had been browsing luxury hotels in Lagos. With Mr Charles out of the country it was the perfect opportunity to take the woman he loved out, he could put business out of mind, and give himself over to her. Quivering fingertips he came across the Hotel Bon Voyage on Victoria Island: Stunning views across the Gulf of Guinea and comfortably distant from both his and Charles respective offices.

Deluxe room with a Lagoon View; ideal. His mobile vibrated into life, it was her:

'Hello.'
'Hey, Mr Charles has gone. I watched his car all the way down the road. He is surely gone. Would you like to come over?'
'No.'
'What?!'
'Ha, I'm joking. But seriously I'm not gonna come round.'
'What you playing at Mike?'
'Pack a night bag honey, I'm taking you out for the night.'
'Oh Mike, that sounds incredible.' She shrieked.
'I'll pick you up in a half hour?'
'Get out of here Mike, you jerk, I need an hour and a half to get ready for you. Minimum!'
'Forty five minutes then.'
'C'mon Mike.'
'An Hour!?'
'Mike are you serious, did you hear me before? Because you don't appear to have heard me?' Her voice now sounded strained.
'An hour fifteen?' Mike continued, enjoying the interchange's absurd whimsy.
'Mike. An hour and half, or I don't know.'
'Ok, I'll pick you up in an hour an a half.' Mike interrupted, putting on a crude Chicagoan accent – Capone style – knowing he would get a laugh: 'Anyways I gots to has a showerz!'

Michael could hear Mrs Charles laughing as he hung up the phone. He'd already had a shower.

He opened the long mirrored sliding doors of his bedroom wardrobe and pulled out a casual navy blue Ralph Lauren suit and a putty coloured shirt. It would be waiting for him there on the bed when he returned from his shave.

An hour later Mr Creek was pulling into the drive of Mr Charles mansion.

He'd turned up fifteen minutes early to accommodate his slow man routine: A stupid joke that he played once in a while, she always seemed to find it very amusing. His plan of action; he would take roughly fifteen minutes to turn off the ignition, check his appearance in the rear view mirror, get out of the car, close the door and lock it and walk up the drive way. If he was in luck Mrs Charles would catch a glimpse of this routine from her bedroom window at the front of the house, overlooking the driveway. Perfect. As he was slow walking up the drive way five minutes later, every snail step deliberate and thoughtful as if walking on an icy lake, he heard the door open in front of him and began raising his head, slowly.

He spoke as if in a black hole 'Hello my darling.'

'Michael, what are you doing standing out in the driveway?' Said the beautiful Mrs Charles, giggling. 'I've come to pick you up,' Michael said, extending the length of his words further, almost singing. Mrs Charles approached him and put one hand on his shoulder. 'How can I cure you?' She asked. 'Just one kiss.' He eventually replied. 'Well I don't know about that Mr Creek.' She said turning as if to go back inside. Mr Creek's slow routine broke and he grabbed her arm twirling her neatly into a passionate embrace.

$$

Mr Creek turned off the Ahmadu Bello Road and down into the underground car-park of the Hotel Bon Voyage. Mrs Charles squeezed his leg and Mr Creek turned to look at her, not noticing the lift open, revealing a tall heavy set man dressed in black. Creek turned through the warren of hibernating vehicles and found a space next to a brand new acid green Lamborghini Gallardo. After parking his silver BMW, he got out of the car, careful not to scratch the translucent perfection of the Lamborghini, and walked around to the passenger side, opening the door for Mrs Charles.

'Ok, here we are. The underground car park of the Hotel Bon Voyage. Simply beautiful isn't it?' He said facetiously as they stood in the dark and dank petroleum perfumed concrete arena. 'I booked us a deluxe room with a great view of the lagoon, well I hope it's great. I haven't seen it before. Anyway pass me your bag won't you?' Mrs Charles reached out a slender arm into the back seat of the saloon car, grabbing her khaki green, and brown leather strapped bag. 'Thankyou Mike.'
'Jesus, what have you got in here?! Why have you packed bricks? You crazy.'
'Shut up Mike, lets go!' She craned her neck, pecking him on his cheek before linking arms and gesturing towards the lift.

'Wait darling, I need to lock the car.' As Michael turned to lock his BMW he caught a glimpse of a dark figure staring in his direction in the silver paintwork of the vehicle. The warp effect of light hitting the curved chassis was disorienting and Mike spun round trying to work out where he could have seen that figure. He squinted into the deepest corners of the carpark and scrutinised the stationary shadows of inanimate vehicles.
'What's wrong, come on I want to see this place.'
'Quiet, wait!' Mike stood still, cursing his short-sightedness. Just as he was about to chastise himself for his paranoia, he felt a heavy blunt object hit the back of his head. It knocked him to his knees and threw him off balance. As his blurred vision struggled to make sense of up and down and right and left, he saw the figure, a freak amalgam of abstract light reflection and Mrs Charles, arms outstretched remonstrating: 'What the fuck! You asshole! Michael! Baby!'

He tried to respond, but struggled to work out how to compel speech. Mouthing silently, he swivelled to face his attacker. Blur: His vision was more skewed than the psychedelic reflections of the recently buffed up silver BMW.

'Fucking stay down, you motherless fuck.' The cold hard butt of the assassin's revolver came down hard between Michael's eyes. He had the peculiar feeling of there being someone inside his head watching his life like a TV show; suddenly deciding to turn the off switch on the remote control of consciousness. As if the station had cut the feed he felt a brief moment of bodily static before black intangible nothingness.

$$$

The laminated cardboard sign red 'Mr Charles.' The letters bold black impact font flared up as the intense sunlight hit the translucent plastic surface.
'Ah look Mr Charles, they've laid on a private car for us, you must be some kind of celebrity.' Said Mr Charles travelling companion, Paul Agahbi, patronisingly.
'Well yes, I am a powerful man, what do you expect.'
'A legend in your own lunchtime Mr Charles, I am truly proud to be lawyer to a man of such repute.' Agahbi patted his his elderly client on the head, ruffling his silver greased hair.
'Enough of that Paul, we have a serious meeting to attend.' Charles spoke dryly. 'Presentation is everything.' Mr Charles smoothed his feathers back, like a peacock, plumage resplendent in the sunlight.

They approached the man with the sign. Black suit, black hat, black sunglasses. The Man smiled, revealing 2. rakish gold teeth and led the businessmen to the vehicle, a black Mercedes benz with blacked out windows.
The car was cool and the atmosphere was thin, the air conditioning had combined with the valet clean leather to create a mobile Himalayan micro climate in the back seat of a luxury German saloon car, the perfume was intoxicating. As Charles and Agahbi settled into their seats the driver spoke with a weird American accent through the intercom:

'As requested there is a bottle of Dom Perignon in the cooler with two glasses, I will now escort you to the Diamond and Gold Mining Corporation Head Quarters. The journey will take approximately an hour and forty five minutes. Sit back and enjoy the ride.'

Agahbi laughed long and loud at the overwhelming atmosphere of American excess as he plucked the ornate champagne bottle from the mini fridge positioned in between the two passenger seats. Handily the top surface of the mini fridge also functioned as a table on which there perched two champagne flutes which stood securely in two ergonomic inlays. It was as if the car was putty, melding to Charles and Agahbi's every need.

Agahbi looked at the bottle in his hands for a moment, analysing the devilish horns of the label before ripping off the foil capsule and popping the cork.

'It looks like they really want your investment Charles, all five million of it.' Agahbi said, sipping his champagne,
'Well who wouldn't with a figure like that.' Charles replied, confident in the fact that he was the master of his own destiny.
'They've really laid it on, can we expect any females to be included in this package, maybe stored in a fridge back at the hotel? Is that how this works?'
'I couldn't possibly say Paul, I have seen a lot in my time here in Africa.'
'What are you trying to say Charles? I resent your insinuation.' Agahbi said thrusting his champagne flute in the direction of Charles' throat, fencing style.
'Nothing Agahbi, merely that I have learnt to expect the unexpected here.' Agahbi retorted; 'Is that why you wanted to come to this country in the first place? The movies didn't thrill you enough? You needed to see a real action movie? Mr Charles. Mr super-hero. Mr Tom fucking Cruise. Hah, you scientologist prick.'

They laughed and clinked their glasses together vigorously as the car sped away from the city out into the dusty plains.

$$$

Benjamin Suma looked down into the empty quarry. He kicked a stone hard and watched it fly over the precipice and bounce ten times before settling at the
bottom of the muddy pit.

It had been three days since he had helped in the messy evacuation of the mine's workers. They had closed the mine after a series of assaults from R U F rebels which they had barely held off. He raised his binoculars to his face and stared at the horizon.

He could see the beautiful lustre of the green forests in the distance. He focused back on closer planes, the dehydrated red earth of the mining territory. The extreme contrast between these two environs made him feel thirsty. He low ered the binoculars letting them hang heavy around his neck again and pulled up his grubby canvas lined canteen from the floor. He undid the cap and drank deeply before pulling the lenses back up to his eyes and twisting them for a moment to clarify the blur. Quickly scanning the perimeter of the mine he noticed a pillar of dust billowing on the highway. He zoomed in, clearly recognising the neat outlined shadows of military grade weaponry mounted on an open-backed jeep moving at a furious pace. Only now remembering his radio, he felt his stomach turn inwards with the realisation of his mindlessness. He sprinted back towards his post and scrambled up into the crows nest of the look-out tower. He quickly grabbed the receiver and pushed the button for transmission:

'Red Alert Red Alert, Combatant's approaching from the north, headed for the north gate, estimated arrival in 2 minutes, take up defensive positions immediately.'

He sounded the alarm hearing the dull drone revolving below him and repeated his message. He watched as the soldiers scurried into position, searching for his father, General Asbenjamin. Finally he found his father, dressed in proud military regalia, arms astray directing troops like a conductor. Dr Marculey the aging director of the gold and diamond mining corporation burst forth from his porta-cabin office, rushing down the small steel steps and over towards General Asbenjamin. The director was dressed in a shirt and khaki trousers, his casual attire now covered in the clouds of dust kicked up around him by the soldiers. The director grabbed Asbenjamin by the elbow and slapped him on the back angrily. From his look out post Benjamin could see them shouting at one another, the soldiers would struggle to organise themselves effectively without the general's guidance. The knot in Benjamin's stomach grew ever tighter, he could not believe the chaos that was playing out before him, they had rehearsed this scenario endlessly but now it seemed as if the players had all forgotten their roles. The first shots rang out at the gate, Benjamin saw Dr Marculey lead his father into the porta-cabin. Not knowing what this meant he strapped the radio pack onto his shoulders, grabbed his M16 and charged down the ladder to the red earth below. He stuck close to the rim of the crater and sprinted down the bank towards the braying gun rattle. He found four of the other look outs at a heavy machine-gun vantage point cut into the bank of the quarry west of the skirmish. He skidded into prone position alongside the other soldiers and began to fire on the armoured vehicle. Raising his binoculars to his eyes he scanned the horizon and saw three other dust clouds hurricaning towards them.

The R U F soldier manning the DShK heavy machine gun mounted on the first jeep was cutting through the soldiers on the walls of the quarry mercilessly. Benjamin could hardly bear to watch. He stood up and made off for the gate, the bellows of his partners at the vantage point bouncing around the quarry walls. 'What are you doin!? Don't break rank!' A piercing noise tore through the air around Benjamin's head as the rocket propelled grenade sped towards its final destination. It smashed the machine gun outpost to smithereens. The projectile had passed just meters from Benjamin's head as he ran towards the gate. Shrapnel fell around him like confetti. He didn't turn back. Closer now he could see that something had gone horribly wrong on the other side of the quarry, there were streams of desperate looking men charging through the forecourt of the mining camp. They must have taken out the western look-out before he had a chance to report the advance of the second group.

Benjamin, listening to the sounds of gunfire, fell to his knees behind a rocky outcrop. Soon enough the percussive echoes of the government M16's diminished and were overridden by the frantic thrashing snarls of the rebel's miscellany of automated weaponry. Cacophony turned into abhorrent peace: Benjamin realising his own powerlessness fell to his knees. His thoughts turned to his father. He brought the binoculars back up from his chest and sought out the porta-cabin. He held his breath and his mind reeled with the possibilities of what could occur. In that moment he insulted himself for knowing that his father would soon be dead. He watched, in a wash of day jah voo as a skinny man in a vest, wearing sunglasses and a cowboy hat dragged his father by the scalp through the door of the cabin and into the dust, followed by another man who kicked Dr Marculey down the hard steel steps. Doctor Marculey fell awkwardly into the dirt, face down. The skinny man pulled Benjamin's father stiffly upright on his knees and spat some inaudible order into his face. The general raised his hands to the back of his head; his face hung solemnly low and his expression impossible to read. A shot rang out filling the quarry with a dozen replicas. His father flinched, Dr Marculey was dead. Benjamin could taste acid bile on his tongue as his saliva ducts went into overdrive. The skinny man fired a shot between General Asbenjamin's eyes. Benjamin's stomach gave way and his father dropped to the ground like a doll.

$$$

Benjamin did not wait to be discovered. He made his way carefully back to his outpost. He wheeled his motorbike quietly away from the quarry before kicking it into life and bursting away from the mine and away from the massacre.

The wind dried the tears on his cheeks, leaving a river delta on his dust encrusted face. He focused on the road and accelerated. About four miles away from the mine he noticed a column of smoke ripping up into the sky like a flare. Wary as he advanced towards it he slowed his vehicle and with one hand held his binoculars to spy a black Mercedes benz, deserted and on fire. He resumed his course approaching the burning saloon. A man stumbled into view, emerging from a roadside ditch, on the opposite side of the road to the car. Clearly unarmed and clearly injured, the man waved his hands pleading for aid. Benjamin slowed and warily approached.

'Help me sir, please help me. I'm all alone here and I am injured in the leg. Can you not see? I cannot walk.' The Nigerian man exclaimed frantically. 'What has happened? Was it the R U F ?'
'I have no idea sir. We were trapped like dogs. Mr Charles fought most of them off. With a half full bottle of vintage champagne! Would you believe it? My flute did not do much damage I have to say, it was rather like fighting with a child's toy machete' Benjamin unable to rationalise the ramblings of the lost man allowed him to continue. The cartoon narrative seeming totally alien to what he had recently experienced.
'Charles cracked one over the head, and the wine gushed into the open wound as the blood rushed out. Anyway he grabbed a gun and left in their jeep. He was like a 65 year old Rambo with the strength and determination of...well Rambo in his prime I guess.'
'Are you wounded badly?' Benjamin said as he looked at the man's bloodied leg.
'Its not good sir, I tried to escape but only got to the other side of the road. It took me hours! Ya' mind if I hitch a ride with you? The hospitality is not much good here in this roadside ditch. Not what I'm used to anyway. Hah.'
'Hop on com paah dray. I've been through some shit too. I'm headed to someone's place who should be able to help you out. Come on.'
'Excuse me, I can't hop anywhere. My leg is fucked in case you haven't noticed. That is not to say that I don't appreciate your very kind offer. Could you give me a hand?'

Benjamin put the bike into standing position, dismounted and helped the fat man up to his feet. Agahbi, using Benjamin as a crutch, hobbled to the bike and with a great effort swung his injured leg over the seat. 'Fuck me, that hurts bad. Now if you're gonna have your ass in my crotch, near my dick, well to be frank I'm gonna need to know your name. Ha. What's your name sir?'

Unresponsive to the man's coarse humour Benjamin responded blankly.

'I am Benjamin Suma, the son of the late General Asbenjamin of Sierra Leone. And who are you?' He said, sitting on the pocked leather seat in front of the wounded man.
'Paul, Fucking, Agahbi. That is who I am. Survivor; hero; legend; attorney at law; family man. Now, where are we going partner?'
'We are going to see an Edith Marculey, a nurse, who is also the wife of Dr Marculey. You see Dr Marculey was just killed at the mine by the R U F. Along with my father. I should let Edith know this. And I'm sure she will be able to have a look at your wound,' Benjamin explained, inwardly surprised at his numbness towards the recent tragedy.
'My father today informed me of his will. That is something else I need to consider. Especially now I am on the run.'
'Now, that is a story. I like the bit about the nurse. Anyway, you know, taxes on inheritance are unusually high at the moment. Perhaps you could use my services. You know my rates are very competitive? I should have a business card somewhere around here,' he said, fumbling at the inside pocket of his inappropriately cream suit.
'I don't want to talk about that now. Be quiet. Let me drive.'
'Fine Ben, just something to think about eh.'

Paul stopped talking, and the road unravelled promiscuously before them as the sun came down low washing the scene in golden light.

$$$

When they arrived at the Marculey residence the sun was down. The scene in front of the ivy sheathed house was illuminated by a security floodlight as Benjamin lurched Paul up the asphalt driveway. The curtains were drawn in the front room, but the light was on. With a heroic effort Benjamin shimmied Paul onto the stoop and rung the doorbell.

'Who is it?' An angelic voice sang.
'It is Benjamin Suma, son of General Asbenjamin. A close aide to your husband. Please let us in. We have very urgent news.'

The door creaked open after the security chain was removed. Edith Marculey was revealed wearing tight fitting jeans and a cornflower blue company t-shirt bearing the familiar hammer and jewel logo of the Sierra Leone National Diamond and Gold Mining Corporation. She hurriedly gestured them into the house. Paul's bleeding leg stained the white carpet.
'Sorry, my leg is bleeding. It likes your carpet no more than it likes my cream suit. Allow me to introduce myself: I'm Paul Agahbi, and this is Benjamin Suma.'
'Yes I know Benjamin well.'

It was painfully obvious to Edith that something serious was wrong, something far and beyond the Nigerian man's leg. Strangely distant from the situation her mind was taken over with an acute anxiety about what could have happened.

'Please Mrs Marculey, can you help him. He has been shot by the R U F, and is presumably a little delirious.'
'Of course, please come into the kitchen, I should have some bandages and antiseptic in there. Is the bullet still in your leg?'
'No it is not. It passed right through. Like a kernel of sweetcorn. Haha ha ha hahaha. Excuse my crude humour maam. Its helping me deal with the pain.'
They helped Paul into the kitchen and sat him down on an oak Provensall kitchen chair.
'Fuck me,' Paul exclaimed as he low erred his weight onto the hard wooden seat and Benjamin filled a bowl with warm water.
'Undo your belt Paul, we are going to have to take your trousers off,' She said snapping open a first aid box.

Paul obliged, relishing the opportunity to quip, 'Does this come with a happy ending?'

'What on earth do you mean you funny man?' She barely laughed as she removed his trousers carefully revealing a mess of gore. Unflinching she cleaned the wound methodically.

'While I'm doing this Benjamin, you said you had urgent news?'

'Yes I'm sorry, well, this is hard for me to say. Your husband was caught up in an attack by the R U F at the mine. I'm afraid that he was killed in the defence along with my father and scores of soldiers. I came here immediately to tell you. Your life may be in danger as well,' Benjamin said staring at the terracotta tile floor.

Edith Marculey, unresponsive, continued to clean Paul's leg. Finishing up, she bandaged the leg tightly. Only then did she fall to her knees with her head in her hands. Neither men knew what to say.

$$

Benjamin Suma scooped the steaming groundnut stew into three bowls, each containing a heap of rice. The rice mound poked through the surface of the red liquor like the tip of an iceberg. He carried the bowls over to the table, returning to the counter to pick up a bottle of home-made ginger beer and poured three glasses. The once ebullient Paul Agahbi was silent, his eyes cast downwards, scrutinizing the floral pattern of the table cloth closely. Benjamin placed a bowl in front of Mrs Marculey, only for it to be pushed away slowly with the back of her hand.

'If there is anything to say in praise of a serious bullet wound, it sure gives you a mighty appetite.'

Paul's nervous humour descended into the silence of the company like a drop falling into a well. Benjamin glanced a steely look at Paul, only now did he realise how little he knew of his new associate.

'What is your business in Sierra Leone anyway Agahbi?'
'I am a Nigerian Lawyer, one of the best in my field. I represent a successful American businessman, Mr Charles, the director of The Chevron International Oil Exploration Corp. We were travelling together to meet Dr Marculey to discuss Mr Charles investment in the Sierra Leone Gold and Diamond Mining Corporation. Marculey had sent a private vehicle to pick us up from the airport, a delightful black Mercedes Benz. Our vehicle was commandeered on root, and the rest is history. What of you Suma? You've said barely anything about what occurred at the mine.'
'Its hard to know how to discuss the execution of your own father. It was right in front,' Benjamin choked. Wiping his eyes to compose himself he fell silent again and spooned the stew into his mouth.
'You must eat, Mrs Marculey.' Said Paul, after swallowing his last spoonful of delicious stew.
'This is probably the last meal I will ever be able to eat in this house, but I just can't stomach it.' Turning to Benjamin, she said: 'I am afraid. I want to leave this place.
'We should both get out of Sierra Leone, there is nothing for us here anymore. Damn this war.'
'Come with me to Nigeria.' Agahbi said. 'You have both saved my life, I can get you the passports, I know people. I am a wealthy man, Though, as I can tell from this beautiful home, so was your husband Mrs Marculey. Forgive

my insensitivity, but do you know of your husbands final wishes regarding his estate.'

'He left me everything. His wealth is partly in property, all of which is lost to the R U F now, but a large proportion, an unimaginable sum, has been secured in an offshore bank account.'

'I know how to secure the wealth ma'am. And you Benjamin, we need to discuss your inheritance as well. It is vital that we move quickly to secure this wealth before it dissapears into the hands of the rebels. Please escort me to Nigeria, I will work on both of your cases for free, it's the least I can do. You have saved my life.'

'I don't think we have any other options. We will leave tonight.'

Edith solemnly nodded her agreement as a single salty tear ran down her cheek.

$$

Mr Charles dry, cracked knuckles gripped the steering wheel tight. They hadn't relaxed since he had taken the jeep and escaped the scene of attack. His nails were digging in to the soft leather and his teeth were clenched. The commandeered M 16 lay on the passenger seat beside him. A broken champagne bottle rolled around in the back seats. The bottle, clinking with every rock the car hit on the dusty Sierra Leone highway, reminded the elderly American of his adrenaline fuelled retaliation. Mr Charles fumbled in the glovebox finding an unmarked cassette tape, wishing for some music to help him concentrate on the road and stop his mind replaying over and over again the surreal attack that had taken place. He slotted it into the tape deck and pushed play. A clatter of drums announced Bruce Springsteen's Born to Run. Mr Charles for the first time relaxed his grip and sat back, comforted by the fortuitous discovery of some strangely ap tuh Americana. Motivated and rejuvenated and now shouting along, Mr Charles was headed back to Nigeria and he wasn't going to stop.

$$

The Ibadan Express Road was wet with the morning rain and there was a timber truck carrying a stack of large raw Mahogany tree trunks racing along the highway. Michael Creek moaned through the gag looking at the unconscious Mrs Charles; her face bruised and beaten. The assassin in the drivers seat shouted; 'Quiet, otherwise I'll silence you right here right now.' As the driver swivelled himself back to face the road his quick jerk knocked a takeaway coffee cup into his lap. The cup was half full and still scalding. He reeled from the burn. This moment of panic, this moment where he took his eyes off the road, turned out to be deadly. A log had come free from its industrial grade steel chain, in an instant it broke from the truck and flew straight through the windscreen pulping the assassin and Michael Creek. Mrs Charles, unknowing, unconscious was incinerated when the vehicles fuel tank exploded soon afterwards. A speeding motorcyclist broke hard as he met the terrible event. Skidding on the wet asphalt and flying free of his vehicle along the surface of the road. Mr Charles, distracted, fists pumping as Born to Run played for the 1000th time, celebrating his arrival in Nigeria, swerved in the last moment before slamming into one of the renegade tree trunks, his car flipping into the air, rolling over and over. The aqua-planeing motorcyclist felt his back break as his body met violently with a sideways log. Sitting slumped against the log he watched helplessly as his own beloved Honda CBR600F flew towards him, gutting him like a fish. Mr Charles flew through the air, ensconced in his metal coffin, screaming with Bruce Springsteen. The vehicle finally came to land, righting itself. Mr Charles sat for a second in a moment of survival and hope before turning to see a huge lorry burning towards him at furious speed. The lorry smashed unrelentingly into the jeep; Charles body was vaporised in the huge explosion. Cars speared themselves on the mahogany logs now scattered all over the highway. One driver found themself unable to brake after a water bottle slid portentously underneath the pedal. The cream saloon made a nose dive into the front end of a log. A red van, gracefully pirouetting as if the principal member of a ballet company performing some freakish danse macabre, limbs flailing from the windows, finally came to rest upside down and contorted at the side of the road. The broken survivors stared out the windows, left cruelly conscious to contemplate the final moments of their lives. They witnessed a customised black corvette slam into the fuel tank of the timber truck, bursting into flames, its driver struggling to escape as he was broiled by the burning fuel. The passengers in the overturned red van watched helplessly as a nightmare lorry thrashed through the wreckage finally laying them all to rest.

$$$

Jo Otumba sat in his office checking his emails when the phone rang.

'Hello, this is Otumba, Provincial Director of the First Bank of Nigeria, Victoria Island Branch. How can I help you?' He said in his particular sing-song phone voice.
'We have some pressing news regarding two of your foremost clients,' a monosyllabic voice answered.
'Can I ask to whom I'm speaking?'
'This Is Detective Guetta.'
'Well detective, good to be speaking to you on this very fine day. Please continue, hummm,' Otumba said as he took a bite out of his lunchtime apple.
'Excuse me sir I'm eating an apple.'
'Quite alright. Anyway I have some unfortunate news regarding a Mr Charles and a Mr Michael Creek. They were killed, April 21st, in a tragic accident on the Ibadan Express Road. I have to say the circumstances were suspicious. Both individuals, and unfortunately Mrs Charles as well, were physically destroyed in the accident. We were able to identify them forensically at the scene, through fragments of teeth and suchlike.'
'Dear god, that is horrific. I don't know what to say.' Jo took another bite of his apple, chewing, comprehending and contemplating.
'Well as I was saying the circumstances were very odd. Very odd indeed. We are not sure why any of the individuals were on the Ibadan Express Road at the time. Mr Charles was driving a jeep with Sierra Leone registered license plates with an M-16 harboured in the vehicle. We know this through verified tooth fragments which were found embedded in the cars steering wheel. Peculiarly, Mr Creek and Mrs Charles have been traced to the same vehicle, as was an individual we already have a record of here in the station. They were in a stolen car. At the moment we speculate kidnapping. We wish to seize the accounts of both Mr Charles and Mr Creek so as to continue the investigation. We need to analyse all financial activity on behalf of these two. The incident I believe demands that.'
'Very well, I will make the necessary arrangements. However I must say that I have had the uptmost respect for both individuals. I find this incident unfathomable.'
'I appreciate your cooperation. We will be in touch.'

'I look forward to it. Goodbye.' Jo hung up the phone and, still gnawing on his apple, began to research his database for details of the Americans and their beneficiaries.

Jo had known Michael Creek, he had even considered him a close friend. Michael held Jo in great confidence, he had discussed his fears concerning his affair with Mrs Charles. Indeed, it was Otumba who had helped the couple find a surrogate family for their illicit love-child, Jani Adams. Furthermore, they had written his last will and testament together in secrecy and 50% of Creek's wealth was to go to Jani, and 50% to Mrs Charles. Otumba was immediately concerned by his conversation with Detective Guetta. He couldn't trust him. The Nigerian police were well known for their insidious corruption. Otumba would make every effort to see that Creek's will was enacted justly. Since Mrs Charles had died in the accident, he would have to find a foreign investor to secure the funds from devolution into the hands of the government. He had to find Jani Adams, but before that he composed an email:

I am Mr. Joseph Otumba, Provincial Director of the First Bank of Nigeria, Victoria Island Branch. I have an urgent and very confidential business proposition for you. On June 6, 2000, an American Oil consultant/contractor with the Nigerian Mining Corporation, Mr Michael Creek made a numbered time (fixed) deposit for twelve calendar months, an unimaginable sum, in my branch. Upon maturity, I sent a routine notification to his forwarding address but got no reply. After a month, we sent a reminder and finally we discovered from his contract employers, the Nigerian Mining Corporation that Mr Michael Creek died from an automobile accident. On further investigation, I found out that he died along with the next of kin detailed in his will.

This unimaginable sum is still sitting in my bank and the interest is being rolled over with the principal sum at the end of each year. No one will ever come forward to claim it. According to Nigerian Law, at the expiration of five years, the money will revert to the ownership of the Nigeria Government, should nobody claim the fund. Consequently my proposal is that I would like you to stand in as the next of kin to Mr Michael Creek, so that the fruits of this man's labour will not get into the hands of corrupt government officials. To make this happen I would like you to immediately provide your full name and address, so that an attorney can prepare the necessary documents and affidavits which will put you in place as the next of kin.

We shall employ the service of two attorneys for drafting and notarization of the will and to obtain the necessary documents and letter of probate/administration in your favour for the transfer. You will provide a bank account which will facilitate the transfer of this money to you, as the beneficiary/next of kin. The money will be paid into your account and you will receive a reasonable percentage. There is no risk at all as the paperwork for this transaction will be done by the attorney and my position as the Branch Manager guarantees the successful execution of this transaction. If you are interested, please reply immediately via the private email address below. Upon your response, I shall then provide you with more details and relevant documents that will help you understand the transaction. Please observe utmost confidentiality. Rest assured this transaction will be most profitable for both of us, because I shall require your assistance to invest my share in your country.

Sincerely

Joseph Otumba

There was still the matter of Mr Charles, and that would be more difficult. He had met the shadowy man only once in person, at a cocktail party. Otumba usually dealt with Mr Charles accounts through his personal lawyer, Paul Agahbi., although reluctantly. Otumba found Agahbi's strange personality offensive and brash.

Otumba worked late into the night trying to find a lead on Charles, some kind of next of kin or a close business connection. Finding nothing he called Agahbi.

"Agahbi?"
"Jo, Jo Jo. How's it going buddy?'
'Not bad Paul, and yourself?' Jo enquired, starting anxiously on another apple.
'Well I have certainly been better, I was shot would you believe in Sierra Leone! I'm ok though, don't worry. I'm currently travelling back to Nigeria. Did you receive my email? I have sent you two drafts of some important documents I will be sending to interested parties overseas very soon. Did you get a chance to read them over for me?'

Jo could hear an engine hum in the background. He quickly opened his gmail account and opened Agahbi's email. The PDF's looked interesting and he quickly consumed their contents.

Dear sir.
I know that my mail might come as a surprise to you because I have not met you before. I came across your contact during my search for a trust worthy partner with the ability to handle a confidential business matter to the benefit of us both.

I am seeking urgent assistance. I would like you to carefully consider this mail and treat the information included as highly confidential.

My name is Madam Edith Marculey, wife to the late Dr Marculey, former director general of the Sierra-leone   Gold and diamond corporation. Sadly, my husband was assassinated by rebels loyal to R U F leader Foday Sankoh. Before his death, he deposited a metallic trunk box containing an unimaginable wealth into a private   security company in Abidjan. The secure box contains a certificate of deposit which states that the beneficiary of   the said consignment was intended to be a foreign business partner based abroad.

My life is now in danger. The R U F will hunt me down and take the consignment if they can. I am currently on the road, fleeing for safety to Nigeria with the documents.

My late husband deposited the box under special arrangement as contaning family valaubles. Thus, the security company does not know the real content of the box. The documents issued to my late husband concerning the transfer of his wealth are readily available and can be sent to you at your request. I am contacting you today to ask for your assistance. As a refugee here I can not open a bank account with my name until my citizenship has been confirmed. I require the support of a foreign agent to help me to claim the box back from the security company and pay it into a bank account here in your name. In exchange I will agree to transfer a reasonable percentage of the amount through any of the international banks for onward transfer to your account.

Yours sincerely,

Madam Edith Marculey.

Otumba scanned the next PDF:

Dear Friend,

My name is Benjamin Suma, son of the late Asbenjamin Suma, a Military General from Sierra Leone. My father was recently executed by R U F rebels in a struggle over the much contested diamond mining territory of my country. I hope that you will take the time to understand the grave nature of my situation and that your empathy may bring both of us some salvation. I have in herited from my father an unimaginable wealth. I have decided to source a neutral assistant to aid me in transferring my fortune out of Sierra Leone and into the US. In exchange for your

assistance I am willing to cut you in on a reasonable percentage of the sum and all
future profits from the investment of my great wealth in your country.

I await your reply.

Yours faithfully,

Benjamin Suma.

'This all looks fine Paul. Good luck to your clients, it seems that they have
been through something terrible. I too have some sad news. Well, Mr
Charles has been killed in a road accident on the Ibadan Express Road. The
police here are trying to seize his accounts and I thought you should
definitely be made aware of this.'
'Oh my god! That bastard, he left me to die! But it got him first. But Jo that
sincerely is tragic news. What of his wife, have you spoken to her? Poor
woman.'
'Dead also, same incident. And Michael Creek. The whole enterprise. I do not
have the time to go into the details. I am sure you will find out eventually .
But I was hoping to pass on the dealings of Mr Charles' accounts to you. I
feel your personal relationship demands it.'
'Thank you Jo for letting me know. I will be more than willing to do this. I will
be in touch when I'm back in Lagos.'
'Ok, well till then Paul.'
'Aye, till then.'
The static turned to silence and Jo laid his head to rest on the keyboard. It
submitted to his face like a crude memory foam pillow. The screen cried:
43weeeeeeeeeeeee3w.

$$

Jani Adams was eating cheerios with a fork and playing an online flash game on her white Sony Vaio laptop, a birthday gift from Michael Creek. She was dressed in her relaxing clothes; a tracksuit and vest. Her school books lay untouched in her bag underneath a heap of uniform in the living room. She hated homework. Her mother was washing up and singing to herself. She stopped and yelled through the thin plaster wall:

'Have you got homework to do?'
'I'm doing it mom!' Jani shouted back, as she killed the cast of American Idol with a 7 inch record.
'You better be, we are going to church in an hour or so.'
'Oh mom, gawd, alright already. I'm doing it. Jesus.' She snapped back, trying to escape a giant Gene Simmons flailing an axe.
'Don't talk to me like that Jani. You have been getting some attitude lately young lady.' Jani's mother was now standing at the doorway to the living room, seeing that Jani was not in fact doing her homework. Then the doorbell rang.
'I'll get it!'

Jani rushed off her seat and darted past her mother to the door. Checking the peephole before unlocking the security chain she saw a peculiar looking individual.

'Who is it?' She shouted through the door.
'My name is Jo Otumba, I have some urgent information for you and your family.'
'Who are you though?' Not waiting for a response she turned and shouted to her mother; 'Mom, there is a man here to see me!'
'Well, I am the President of the First Bank of Nigeria, Victoria Island Branch. Please let me in.'

Waiting for her mother's nod of approval Jani unlocked and opened the door.

'Come in come in, would you like some tea?'
'No thankyou, I need to make this brief. From this moment onwards your life will never be the same.'

'What are you going to do to me?' Jani asked.

'I think you need be seated Jani, and your mother too.' Jani and her mother led the man to the living room and sat down.

'I have some very sad news. Michael Creek is dead.' Jani's mother gasped and put her head in her hands. Jani looked at the man with an expression of perplexed sadness.

'Jani, I am here to inform you that Mr Creek declared in his last will and testament that you should receive 50% of his estate. The other 50% was to go to a Mrs Charles. However Mrs Charles died in the same accident which killed Mr Creek. As such all of his estate is now yours. It's an unimaginable sum I must say.'

'What? I don't believe you. This is crazy! Why would he do that? Crazy jesus.'

'Jani, there's something we need to tell you. I should have told you a long time ago. But there never seemed an appropriate moment. Its so sad how I have to tell you right now.'

Jani's mother said, raising her face from the floral meadow of her thin cotton dress.

'What is it mom, what is it?'

Jani could feel a nervous energy whynd and coil up into a large, suffocating ball inside of her.

'Well, I am not your, well I am, but I am not your, biological mother. Your father is not your biological father. Mr Creek and Mrs Charles are your real parents. We were chosen by them as surrogates. I'm sorry Jani, I'm so sorry.'

Jani's eyes filled with tears and she ran out of the room and then the flat, slamming the door behind her and sprinting down the 12 flights of stairs and into the street below.

When she finally returned to the flat, three hours later, she walked through the living room. Her surrogate mother and father were sat waiting for her. She looked at their sad faces, staring back at her expectantly and burst into tears.

'Oh Jani! We love you more than our lives.' The woman stood and approached her, arms outstretched. Jani brushed her aside, now weeping piteously and ran with one arm covering her eyes, a route she knew blind, landing softly face first into the pillow of her single bed, the door slamming behind her, closed with the force of a well aimed heel kick.

'We have always tried to do what we thought was best for you, within our means, Jani. Please don't hate us over this.' Her mother said through the door.
'Just leave me alone mom.'
Jani heard her mothers footsteps retreating from her bedroom door. Wiping the tears from her eyes, Jani sat up and opened the laptop which was resting on her bedside table. She opened firefox only to be affronted by the flash game she had been enjoying only hours before this crisis. Eeemowgame wasn't funny anymore, it was just shit. She clicked away, opened a new window and logged in to her Gmail account.

New message: She began to type.

My beloved,

It is my pleasure to contact you for a business venture which I intend to establish in your country. Though I have not met with you before, I believe that sometimes one has to risk confiding in a stranger to succeed.

I have recently inherited an unimaginable fortune from my father. He wanted to use this money for his political ambitions in our country before he was kidnapped and killed by unknown gun men. Both my father and mother are dead and I do not have any hope without their money. This is why I am contacting you today.

I have decided to invest this money in your country for security and political reasons. I thank God for this opportunity but I am truly distraught at what has happened; my father is gone and my family are all dead.

This investment shall be made in your company upon your withdrawal of the consignment. I do not have the means to work on this, and will commit suicide if I cannot secure my father's treasure.

I want you to help me claim and receive the consignment which will be sent to you through diplomatic means to your address. This will avoid any trace of the funds and will enable you to make the necessary arrangements for the investment in your country.

I would like to invest part of the money into these three areas. But, if there is any other business that you feel more appropriate for my investment then I will be very glad to follow your advice:

1). Real estate
2). The transport industry

3). Five star hotel

If you can be of assistance to me, I would be pleased to offer to you a reasonable percentage of the total fund, whilst the balance will be invested by you. I need all your understanding and honesty to help me at this difficult time. I assure you I will always be your sister.

I await your soonest response.

Respectfully yours,

Miss Jani Adams

$$

Jack was drunk. His suit was crumpled and muddy. He had finished the bottle of whisky as he drove his jeep to the beach house to meet Sarah. He kept replaying the explosion over and over in his mind, knowing also that he would have to tell Sarah about her father's death. Did the Togolese think he was dead? He couldn't be sure of anything, but he assumed so.

He felt relieved when he arrived at the beach house, its pink pastel clapboards glowed in the afternoon sunlight and the gentle sea lapped into warm sand only metres away. Rushing to the screen door, he slapped on the peeling wooden frame. Shouting Sarah's name he realised he was slurring. He quickly tried to compose himself, shoving three pellets of chewing gum into his mouth to disguise whisky breath and vainly patting down his suit. Sarah answered the door.

'Jack, what on earth is wrong? You look a mess.'
'Sarah Sarah, I need to speak to you. Something bad has happened. We are both in trouble!'
'Come in Jack. Oh man you look like you have had a rough time. Jeez. Come in, I'll give you a drink.'

Sarah gestured for Jack to come into the charming kitchen and sit at the dining table. A bottle of cabernet sew vin yon stood opened and half full on the table with an empty glass.

'I'm sorry, I have had a couple of glasses of wine.' Sarah giggled.
'Its ok, I had a drink too.' Jack responded soberly, despite feeling the ground move as he sat down. Sarah poured out two glasses of wine.
'What is it Jack, what is the matter?'
'Your father is dead. I narrowly escaped myself. They probably think I'm dead too, there was an explosion in the coffee shop we were in. I'm so sorry.'
'Oh god. Daddy!' Sarah started to cry, and then screamed 'How did you let this happen?!'
'I'm sorry, I thought we were careful. I'm sorry I brought this violence with me. They may still be hunting me but they will be hunting you now. These are dangerous men, merciless killers. I'm sorry, you have to stick with me now, I will help you.'

Sarah lowered her hands and cried uncontrollably, her chest heaving with every short breath. Jack got up and went to comfort Sarah, he put one arm gently on her back, and looking down her top he whispered into her ear; 'Trust me. We can be safe together.' Sarah removed her shaking hands from her face and wrapped her arms around Jack's midriff. He lowered himself down to look into her eyes; he could see that she was frightened. Sarah tightened her hold and as she moved her head to place it on his shoulder he kissed her lips. Their lips still engaged, Sarah unbuttoned his shirt.

$$

Sarah's head was resting neatly on Jack's chest, one hand stroking his neck and cheek. She started to cry again. Jack held her closer and tried to console her.

'We will be ok. I know a place we can go to in Ghana, we will be safe there for a while. We can arrange to leave the country. We both have enough money now to escape this mess, you will inherit your fathers fortune, it needs to be secured as soon as possible.'
'Yes, my Father was a very wealthy man, my mother is dead, we only had each other in the whole world. He meant everything to me . .' She began to weep into Jack, he held her face and kissed the salty droplets as they fell from her eyes.

$$$

Entering the refugee camp, the widow felt like she was entering some medieval ghetto. She walked along a narrow alleyway and skirted an open sewage ditch. She remembered Ed Wark's advice to stay strong, but now he was dead and she wasn't sure how she would get out of this place. She coughed into her white cotton handkerchief, opening it to reveal flecks of blood. She felt sore and her back ached, despite requesting medical assistance repeatedly, no one had come to see her. She couldn't see any future outside of the camp anymore. On the way back from the medical station she passed tens of dozens of one and two-room houses, each leaning on the other for support. This was a city without streets, sidewalks, gardens, patios, trees, flowers, plazas, or shops, and inhabited by an uprooted, stateless, scattered people in a tragic diaspora. She passed scores of small children, the third generation of refugees born in the camp. .

She entered the door of a dwelling, only distinguishable to her eyes from hundreds of others like it. There were two women on their hands and knees, both in shirts and pants, scrubbing a concrete floor. They rose, one somewhat laboriously, heavy with child, and the other, a young mother of two, a woman made old before her time by endlessly making do in a makeshift home, a home that is only this room with a concrete floor and blankets stacked against the walls for beds. And, for a toilet, a closeted hole in the floor. This woman had never known the convenience of a tub or a commode, nor had any members of her family enjoyed that greatest of all luxuries; a room or even space into which one can for an hour or a few moments of each day retire, and in solitude meld mind, body, and soul.

The widow looked at the heavily pregnant woman: 'Hello Sarah, how are you today?' She asked wearily.
'I'm fine, tired but ok. This one is getting heavy though.' She said rubbing her tulip bulbous tummy. Jack entered behind the widow, his face dark, the shadowy perimeter of his head illuminated by the light of the midday sun. He stole his way in to the half light of the windowless dwelling and pecked Sarah on the cheek. Putting his arm around her he looked to the widow.
'Are you feeling any better?'
'No, they still have not sent anyone to examine me. I am coughing blood now. I feel terrible.'
'Bastards, they must send someone soon. I fear for my child. My son cannot be born here Jack, it can't happen.'

'Sarah, please.'
The silent lady, still scrubbing the floor of their collective home looked up disapprovingly. She shook her head, stood up and walked out into the daylight.
Jack turned to Sarah, 'It will be ok baby, my man came through. I have a surprise for you.'

Jack guided Sarah to their portion of the room as the widow settled into her bed, curled up into a foetal ball.

'Look . . .' Jack said, removing a Mack Book Pro from his khaki knapsack. Sarah pushed the circular switch and the machine began to glow like a deep sea fish in the perennial gloom of the tent. 'I will just log in to the camp Why Fye, and we can begin to send the emails that we have been dreaming of all these months.'
'Oh Jack, finally some hope.'

Jack opened Safari and logged into his hotmail account and clicking new message, he began to type:

Dear Sir,

Permit me to inform you of my desire of going into business. I have aquired your name and contact details from the chamber of commerce and industry. My name is Jack Thompson, the only son of the late King Arawi of Tribal-land. My father was a very wealthy traditional ruler, poisoned to death by his rivals in a conflict over leadership and the distribution of tribal wealth.
Before his death in Togo he called me to his sick bed and confided in me, informing me of a trunk box containing an unimaginable wealth. It was because of this private wealth that he was poisoned by his fellow tribesmen. I have fled my tribe with the riches and I now seek a foreign partner to whom I can transfer the proceeds for investment as you may advise. I am willing to offer you a reasonable percentage of the total sum as a compensation for you efforts, and will provide cover for all of your expenses regarding this matter.

Anticipating to hear from you soon,

Thanks and God Bless

Jack Thompson.

'Ok Sarah that's me. You next. Remember what we talked about?'

'Yes yes I know.' Sarah said as she took the Mack Book and sat it on her lap. She opened up her Gmail account. New Message:

My Dearest,

With deep sorrow and tears in my eyes I write to you. I know that this message might come to you as a surprise because we have not met each other before. I am Sarah Angbozan, 24 years old, and the only daughter of the late Dr. Angbozan Wattra; a successful business man. He was an importer and exporter of Cocoa during his life time, but he was killed in a recent crisis in Cote d'Ivoire. All his properties were totally destroyed.

My father deposited money in the A D B Bank of Burkina Faso with my name as the next of kin. I wish to request your assistance in investing this sum in a lucrative venture perhaps a manufacturing or real estate management project in your country.

The Amount stored in A D B Bank is unimaginable. I need you to help me begin my investment in your country. I require your assistance in the transferral of the fund to an account in your country. My father was warned by his bankers before he died that this would be the only way to successfully export our financial interests overseas.

The bank will not release the money to me until I am 30 years old so I urgently require someone who will stand as my trustee to enable the bank transfer. I will gladly give you some reasonable percent from the total sum for your assistance. It is important you contact me immediately to clarify the next step so we can reach a smooth conclusion. Also I would like to move to your country following this procedure; you could help me look for a good university where I can complete my studies.

Awaiting your immediate response,

Thanks for your understanding,

Yours Sincerely,

Miss Sarah Angbozan,

As Sarah's elegant fingers executed the finishing key strokes to her pleading email, a man and a woman dressed in white and green flapped their way into the tent.

'The Widow, where is the Widow. The Liberian.'

Jack gestured to the pile of cloth and fleece in the corner. The white men rushed to the mound and carefully removed the now unconscious widow from her sleeping nest. Her skin seemed unusually translucent, her face twisted into a yellow mask of pain as the ambulance warden carried her from the tent in his arms. The green lady began to gather some of the woman's belongings together into a bag before she too followed her partner out of the tent, into the ambulance and away.

$$

Dr Muhammed Lucien was doing his daily rounds. He had twenty-two patients. Some seriously ill and some less so. But, they all needed, and he hoped, all depended on his attention. He was a kind man, with generous eyes. He was always willing to listen to the stories of his patients. He had certainly heard some stories: The Sahara Clinic took individuals from all over the continent. A lot came from refugee camps, and sought survival within these seaweed sanitised white walls. They were the only respiratory specialist institution in West Africa. He leant back in his humble desk chair, smiling silently to himself. He stood up, whirled his white coat into place around his shoulders, whipped his stethoscope around his neck and slid a biro pen into the breast pocket of his coat. A red, plastic leather folder lay on his desk, shining up at him in the mid morning sun; the last piece of his routine. As he strolled the corridors of the hospital, greeting the nurses with a kind smile and a frivolous wink he flipped through his log. He came to The Widow's page and stopped. A nurse had spoken to him earlier, informing him that the Widow had been fully conscious early that morning, even eating a little breakfast. Her blood pressure had finally stabilised. He looked forward to meeting her properly. The bronchitis had nearly killed her but the emergency crew had pulled her out of the camp just in time.

It was late in the afternoon when he finally made it to the widow's bedside. Approaching her portion of the ward he saw her closed eyes and assumed she was sleeping. Unclipping her status book from the metal frame at the bottom of her bed he opened it. It seemed that she was doing much better. When he raised his eyes from the paper The Widow's eyes were open. She smiled a tiny smile and began to speak quietly.

'Doctor, thank you, you have saved my life.'
'Not at all, I didn't do much really, just a few tweaks here and there.' Muhammed smiled. 'You are strong, you have fought this all by yourself My Dear.'
'Well I couldn't have done it without you. Please will you let me hold your hand.'
'Of course,' Muhammed replied, sitting down beside her and placing his hand in hers.
'How are you feeling?'
'Much better thank you. I feel like I am getting stronger, my mind feels clearer.'

'Yes, that will be because we have taken you off of the morphine now. It takes a while for the foggy feeling to clear.'
'Doctor . . . ' The widow squeezed Muhammed's hand and held on tightly. 'I am sorry to burden you, but I need to speak to somebody about this. I am in turmoil about my future, the worry is with me day and night. I need to relieve my mind, can I confide in you?'
'Of course my dear, what is the matter?'

The widow explained the entire story of her husbands death at the hands of the Liberian ex-warlords, the bones of his body perhaps still lying crumpled in the market place. She described the unimaginable wealth she had inherited and the way that she had fled the country with the aid of the U N, entrusting her inheritance to Ed Wark the American agent, after his visit to her home to investigate an illicit arms dealer. She described their discussion in her living room in Monrovia over a long camp aahree in the warm Liberian dusk and wept with the fate of her fortune.

'But now, Wark is dead, and there is nothing I can do. I received the message by mail from his office a month ago. It seems that my dear friend Mr Wark was killed in a major Indonesian earthquake. Here . . .' She removed a neatly folded, cream document from the bag at her bedside.
'The letter states that he returned to the U S. Apparently his investigation was stopped by an American government agency just before he could subpoena the dealers.'
'That truly is a tragedy' The doctor said, scanning the letter, confirming the details.
The widow continued: 'He had to return briefly to a government office in Texas to finalise the cancellation of his investigation. That's when I received the first letter . . .' The widow produced another smaller, crumpled piece of paper from her bag.
'He says here that he put my inheritance into a security deposit box at the First National Bank of Texas for safe keeping. He includes the details of the account, the name of a trustworthy contact and a passcode. I am a rich woman Muhammed, I will pay you handsomely if you can help me to secure my fortune and leave this continent.'
'But what happened to Wark?'
'The letter says that he was re-assigned to a U.N project in Indonesia, in Bali. He was killed in an earthquake. That is all I know. Will you help me?'
'I will, but I think we should find an investor for your money. I know just what to do.'

The doctor gently removed his hand from the Widow's own, stood up and walked to the next bed. Felicity Nabassa was reading a pamphlet for an Australian forest fires charity when the doctor approached.

'Hello Felicity, how are you feeling.'
'I am getting weaker doctor, I can feel it.'
'Felicity, we can beat this, stay strong.'
'I am trying doctor, what can I say.'
'I will be back in a moment my dear, but could I ask you to lend me your computer briefly? The Widow in the next bed would like me to help her to write an email to a relative.'
'Of course Doctor, you know you are too kind.'
'Thank you Felicity,' the doctor said, pulling the MacBook pro from Felicities Louis Vuitton hand bag and returning to the Widow's bedside.

'Ok' Muhammed said, sitting himself down close to the bedside and stretching his arms out, his fingers woven together and bending backwards. He opened the computer on his lap:

Dear Sir,

My name is Dr Mohamed Lucien, a medical Doctor and the sole proprietor of the Respiratory Specialist Hospital; Sahara Clinic and Maternity, in Accra Ghana. I understand that an anonymous email is probably not the best way to contact you because of the confidentiality which my proposal demands, but time is of the essence in this case. I hope you understand.

I have a widow here in my clinic. She is on political asylum from Liberia and currently staying at the Accra, Ghana, and West African Refugee Camp. She has been seriously ill for some months now and is currently in the hospital being treated for chronic bronchitis.

This woman has confided in me based on the free medical attention I have been giving to her. She has revealed to me certain details about her late husband, and the repercussions of her tale could be of some interest to you. Her husband was a top government military officer in Liberia during the civil war. He was assassinated a few months ago in a revenge killing enacted by soldiers loyal to a former warlord and enemy of the government whilst shopping in a market-place in Monrovia.

My patient has inherited an unimaginable fortune from her late husband. She has asked me to source a credible and trustworthy partner abroad who will manage her funds for investment.

After her husbands death The Widow was visited by an American U.N official named Edward Wark. Wark was searching for leads on a suspected gun-runner. On hearing the news of The Top Military Officer's death he offered to help my patient secure her new wealth in the U S and find a way of securing her emigration there. However, Ed Wark's arms dealing investigation was cancelled under suspicious circumstances and he was re-assigned to a U.N project in Indonesia. Unfortunately Ed Wark was recently killed in a major earthquake on the island of Bali. He had however secured the widow's inheritance in an account in Texas prior to his departure for the South Seas.

And so it is that I implore you, in the name of Allah, to take up Ed Wark's post and aid my patient in clearing the consignments with the American officials. Confidentiality is imperative in this case. If U.S customs were to realise the origin of this consignment, their suspicions would likely result in the removal of the wealth and the cancellation of its potential for investment, thus leaving The Widow stranded here in the refugee camp, a fate that would most certainly kill her before her time.

We believe in you. We know that you are confident and ready to take on this responsibility, to help us manage this large sum, to the profit of all involved. We also need to establish some way of creating a new home for The Widow in the U.S where her illness can be better treated.

After she disclosed this information to me, I requested that she entrust to me all the documents relating to this deposit. I now have these documents secured and I will not hesitate to fax to you the copies as a proof for your inspection as soon as we receive your response to this email. I am obliged to assist this lady. I know that her business knowledge is limited and as such she can not manage this fund herself, alone in Africa.

In order to avoid any trace of her by the government, I need to trust that we have a mutual understanding. After I am satisfied with your honesty we shall make plans on how the funds can be secured into an account in your name, after which you will arrange to travel immediately to meet with the bank for clearance. The unimaginable wealth is contained in a sealed safety deposit box and it is registered and declared as containing family treasures and precious items. As far as I am aware the bank do not know that there is cash money in the box.

Allow me to assure you that this transaction is 100% risk free and from my discussions with The Widow, we have agreed to give you a reasonable percentage of the total sum for your involvement and assistance. We can discuss this further upon our receipt of your quick response.

Thanks, and God bless you for your understanding,

Best regards,

Dr Mohamed Lucien.
00233 244 937082

Mohamed clicked the send button. 'It is done,' he said, looking up from the screen. The Widow did not reply. She had fallen into a peaceful sleep, her face seemed calm and contented, like a great weight had been lifted from her body.

Mohammed closed the computer and picked up his red-plastic folder. Opening it up he went about his normal routine, checking the drug levels and heart rate and logging them neatly on the paper form. He smiled as he left The Widows bedside, happy to be helping put such a sick patients mind at ease.

He approached the bedside of Felicity Nahbasa and returned the computer to its case in her handbag.
'Thank you Felicity, the Widow appreciates your help very much.'
'That's ok.' Felicity whispered, her eyes half closed.
'Are you feeling ok?' Muhammed asked placing a hand on her head, his voice echoing in her thickly numbed and doughy mind, booming like an underwater volcano.
'I am sleepy,' she whispered, her eyes closing slowly and tightly as she fell away from the Doctor and into sleep.

$$$

She could smell rising ash in the distance, like a field being burnt on the edge of her childhood village. She was standing in a dusty square surrounded by low, abandoned dwellings with open doors and windows. A huge salt and pepper hunting dog ran across the path that suddenly stretched out in front of her, divided by a line of washing. The bright colours of the chilledrens T-shirts and floral dresses grew ever more strangely mute before her eyes as the skies began to grey. The hunting dog's long dripping tongue hung out between its yellow teeth, panting heavily as it turned to look at her for a moment before the wind suddenly whisked all the clothing from the lines and thrust them into the dirt at her feet. The dog calmly turned back and continued to trot its course through the village.

Only then did Felicity realise why the world was growing so dark around her – she could see a huge, wide wall of thick black smoke rising like stretched molasses above the houses surrounding the square. She tried but couldn't move. She was nowhere. She could see the faces of her mother, her father and her dead husband moving in the smoke as it gathered around her. They grasped for her as she reached out her hand. Soft touches tickled the tips of her fingers, a kiss on her wrist and then the heat as the flames enveloped the whole of her again.

$$$$$$$$$$$$$$$$$$$$$$$$$$$
$$$$$$$$$$$$$$$$$$$$$$$$$$$
$$$$$$$$$$$$$$$$$$$$$$$$$$$
$$$$$$$$$$$$$$$$$$$$$$$$$$$
$$$$$$$$$$$$$$$$$$$$$$$$$$$
$$$$$$$$$$$$$$$$$$$$$$$$$$$
$$$$$$$$$$$$$$$$$$$$$$$$$$$
$$$$$$$$$$$$$$$$$$$$$$$$$$$
$$$$$$$$$$$$$$$$$$$$$$$$$$$
$$$$$$$$$$$$$$$$$$$$$$$$$$$
$$$$$$$$$$$$$$$$$$$$$$$$$$$
$$$$$$$$$$$$$$$$$$$$$$$$$$$
$$$$$$$$$$$$$$$$$$$$$$$$$$$
$$$$$

* 9 7 8 1 4 7 1 6 0 0 6 5 4 *